Feed My Sheep
60 Years in Ministry

By Bob Mumford
with Keren Kilgore

LIFECHANGERS®

P.O. Box 3709 ❖ Cookeville, TN 38502
931.520.3730 ❖ lc@lifechangers.org

PLUMBLINE

Published by:

LIFECHANGERS ®
LIBRARY SERIES

P.O. Box 3709 | Cookeville, TN 38502
(800) 521-5676 | www.lifechangers.org

All Rights Reserved
ISBN 978-1-940054-05-6

© 2014 Lifechangers
All Rights Reserved
Printed in the United States of America

Feed My Sheep
60 Years in Ministry
by Bob Mumford

Contents

Feed My Sheep
60 Years in Ministry

by Bob Mumford

Jesus said to him, "Feed My sheep!"
John 21:17

When I came to the Lord, His call on my life was clear, "Feed My sheep!" And, for the past 60 years, I have sought to be faithful to this call to teach others, as openly and vulnerably as possible, what the Lord has so carefully given me to nourish and encourage those to whom He would send me. It has been both a challenge and a joy to discern and produce spiritual food from the Father's table. This journey has involved breaking up religious incrustation, empty tradition, and other unnecessary baggage that has collected over the years, weighing down our ideas of what it means to follow Jesus. We need a philosophy of life that effectively eliminates the false distinction between the religious and secular in our lives. Our responsibilities at home or at the office are no different from our responsibilities to God. Living in the Kingdom causes us to cease thinking in two categories and begin to give back to the Father the one life that He has given us in as pure and free manner as we are capable.

I am exceedingly grateful to the Lord for giving me my wife, Judith, who has been my help-meet and traveling companion for 58 of these 60 years. We have four children who are all walking with the Lord, 32 grandchildren, and 10 great-grandchildren.

2011 | Bob & Judith Mumford

This is a real testimony to the faithfulness of God, especially in light of the fact that I traveled about seventy percent of the time as our children were growing up. I cannot take credit for where they are spiritually; all I can say is that Judith was an excellent mother and God is faithful!

1930s

Many things have changed since I was born in 1930. Judith and I felt like it would be good to share some of the history and events over the past 84 years of my life including how I met the Lord, my time in the United States Navy, my conversion, and the events that led to my entering the ministry in 1954.

I was born in Steubenville, Ohio, the third of eight children. My birth was complicated and when I finally

1932 | Diane and Bob in Roanoake, VA

arrived, I weighed just over 2 pounds and was 21" long. Shortly after birth, I was discovered to have Diphtheria, Cholera, Tuberculosis and severe colic. The frailty and suffering caused my mother to carry me around on a pillow. According to her testimony, she often prayed that I would die to put me out of my misery. Screaming night and day from burning fever and inflammation in my throat and GI tract, my Mother told me she was repeatedly tempted to smother me just to give me some relief. Poverty prevented her from access to the proper medicines, but a compassionate doctor gave my Mom samples of medicine and cans of Eagle Brand Condensed Milk which she fed me with an eye dropper and sustained my life. It was a miracle that I even lived.

I had two brothers who both died as infants. One died before I was born and the other when I was about six years old. We couldn't afford a real funeral service so we had one in the back yard at night so the

2014 | Bob and his sisters, Jean, Peg, and Diane

neighbors wouldn't see. Afterwards, my sister, Diane, and I dug the grave and buried our infant brother in a cardboard shoe box.

I was raised with five sisters—Diane, Peg, Jean, Jane, and Joy—whom I love deeply and often joke of having been raised under petticoat government. Jane and Joy have gone on to be with the Lord.

My father owned a weather stripping and caulking business and allowed me to work for him when I was very young. At seven years old, I used to load the caulking guns for him. Back then, you had to pull the caulking out of

1937 | Bob at 7 years old

the five-gallon cans because they didn't have loaded cylinders.

Our family moved from town to town as my Dad found work and in each place we lived I slept on the sofa, in the attic, basement, on the front porch, or at a neighbor's house while my sisters all shared one room. Our whole family shared one bathroom.

On December 7, 1941, I was 11 and my sister, Diane, was 13. We were sitting in a breakfast booth in Roanoke, Virginia with our Mom and Dad listening to the radio when we heard the unique voice of Franklin Roosevelt announce that a state of war existed between the United States and the Japanese empire. I can remember well my Mom and Dad reacting to the fact that we had just entered the Second World War. The moment I heard we were attacked, I wanted to be

Bob's parents, Margaret and Bernard Mumford

part of what was happening. The American spirit was alive and well and many men signed up, but I was just a boy and was too young to do so.

As a sweaty little 10-year-old kid, I would run the streets with a friend who was just as scrappy and scrawny as I was. One day we happened upon a big Baptist church having a baptismal service and I said to my friend, "Wait here for me; I've got to go in and get baptized." I did not understand what I was doing, but I felt compelled. I ran inside and told them what I wanted to do. The pastor looked at me then asked, "Do you want to be baptized like you are?" When I said yes, he said, "Okay, we'll do that." I got in the water with all my clothes on and afterwards ran out of the church dripping wet. Why they baptized me I still don't understand; the pastor must have had some spiritual perception. I didn't even know the Lord then; I didn't meet Him until I was 12 years old.

I began seeing how people act in their own self-interest one evening at the dinner table. My Dad, Grandpa, and I were sitting at the family dinner table and there was one pork chop left on the serving plate. No one wanted to take it. There was a bad storm outside and suddenly lightening hit and the lights went out. As soon as it was dark, my Dad and my Grandpa both went for the pork chop. Grandpa beat him to it, my Dad stuck his fork in my grandfather's hand, and all hell broke loose. As a young boy, I didn't know what happened, but the anger and fighting that ensued when the lights came back on really shook me. That terrible dinner was quickly over; we packed up and left my grandfather's house.

I didn't understand what was going on because both of them were Christians. Now I know that both of them were moving in their own self-interest. A lot happens when the lights go out; I learned that human greed manifests itself in the dark!

Childhood Vows

A year later, my sister, Diane, and I were walking down the street in Roanoke, Virginia and some students from Trevecca Nazarene University in Nashville were playing the guitar and sharing the Lord at a Nazarene evangelistic meeting. We walked into the meeting and were fascinated. Someone asked us if we had the desire to accept the Lord and both of us said yes. They led us in a salvation prayer and it was quite an encounter for me. I felt I had been lifted into a new dimension and was walking a few inches above the ground.

The following day, I went back to work with my Dad and was grinning from ear to ear from this experience. One of my Dad's friends asked me why I was grinning and I told him about the decision I had made to follow Jesus. After that, word spread and all my father's friends and employees were relentlessly making fun of my faith and taunting me. At 12 years old, the persecution caused me to want to forget ever being a Christian. I remembered hearing that if you cursed the name of God or blasphemed the Holy Spirit, His presence would leave you. So one day, I stood in the middle of the street and cursed God hoping that He would leave me alone and all the pressures would cease. My, did it work! For the next 12 years, I walked as a backslider in deep spiritual darkness.

Divorce Court

When I turned 13, we moved to Atlantic City, New Jersey where my parents had serious conflict in their marriage and went through an ugly divorce. My predisposition to understand the difference between the Kingdom as Father and the Church as Mother[1] came from this very painful but enlightening experience.

Early in my 13th year, I found myself in a courtroom with the judge saying, "Son, since I don't see reconciliation as an option, you will need to make a decision as to which parent you want to live with." What I felt was the pressure of choosing which one I believed would take the best care of me. I would never wish that kind of trauma on any child. Thoroughly confused and terribly torn, I chose to stay with my mother. My father's response to this was, "Well, your mother needs you. But you will live long enough to understand the deeper issues." His statement proved to be quite true. Unfortunately, divorces and the loss of family are part of the deep pain of our society.

I made a childhood vow then and there that once I found my mate I would never divorce. After the

[1] The *Plumbline* "The Kingdom as Father and the Church as Mother" © 2009 can be purchased from www.Lifechangers.org. It clarifies the biblical difference between the Kingdom as Father and the Church as Mother. The visible and institutional Church may be facing a terrible shaking, perhaps even a revolution. We may be forced to choose between the Church and the Kingdom. This *Plumbline* will allow us to love the Church, which is His body, and be faithful to her while keeping the Kingdom a priority.

divorce was over and my Dad moved out, I was the only male and found myself accountable for my four sisters, so I took on the role of a surrogate father. It was a joy and never a conscious burden. At the time, my Mom was pregnant with my youngest sister, Joy, so eventually there were five girls for which I was responsible. For two years, I did the best I could to go to Middle School and do odd jobs to help my Mom keep food on the table. Finally, I quit school in the 9th grade and went to work full time.

It wasn't long before the difficulties, willfulness, and aberrations of my mother began to appear to me. Going to the bars to find her late at night became an unpleasant responsibility. I began to see the deeper issues that my father was talking about.

There is no question that we will see the present pressures cause the Church as Mother to seek her own interests (see Phil. 2:21) and preserve her own agenda. We have already lived long enough to see the deeper issues of the unprecedented departure of Mother ignoring and refusing the expectations and principles of the Kingdom of God.

At age 14, I went to visit my father who was living in St. Petersburg, Florida. He was driving me back home to New Jersey and by the time we got to Baltimore, Maryland we were into a heated argument over my mother. As I started to defend her, my Dad stopped the car and said, "Get out." I thought something was wrong with the tires, so I walked around the car checking each of them and then walked over to the driver's side of the car. He rolled down his window and said directly in my face, "You are no good, you never were any good, and you never will be any good." Then he rolled up his window and drove off leaving me standing there, 150 miles from home.

I had no money for food or bus fare, so it took me 8 hours to hitchhike home to Atlantic City. Standing on that street corner, I made a second childhood vow that I would never trust anyone again. Years later, the Lord revealed to me how vows of this kind can be a major stronghold in one's life. It was a long and agonizing journey to get clear with my father. However, in the faithfulness of God, He gave us relational freedom, a real friendship, and restored our father-son relationship.

Fascination with the Navy

As a 15-year-old, I fell in love with the Navy and in the back of my mind was always preparing myself to join. I collected old magazines from the barbershops and I would cut out pictures of ships and paste them into a scrapbook. I began to learn the name, size, and outline of every ship in Navy so that I could identify it on the horizon. My uncle Jack Carhart was in the Navy and encouraged me. He told me a story about being in a gun encasement somewhere in the Atlantic during WWII when the guy beside him secretly lit a cigarette. To avoid the light being seen by the enemy, the captain took his .45 and shot into the

1945 | Bob's Navy scrapbook

tub and the bullet went ping! ping! ping! ricocheting around the tub. He said, "Bob, the guy quickly put out his cigarette; somehow no one was injured, but it was scary!" It amazed me that one man would risk everybody on the ship for a cigarette. Stories like this fascinated me and enforced my manhood. Ages 13 to 16 are crucial years when your manliness is shaped and other than an occasional visit from Uncle Jack, there was little or no male influence in my life.

In 1946 when I was 16 years old, I went to work for Baron Walker, a German engineer who owned a gas station in Pleasantville, New Jersey. He was a male figure in my life and began to mentor me. I don't know what would have happened if, in the sovereignty of God, Father hadn't given me Baron Walker. He began to teach me integrity, honesty, and keeping my word. "We don't make excuses, we make good!" he would often say. Little by little, he gave me responsibility.

One morning a con man came in, did a shuffle on me, and cheated me out of $18. I was sure Baron Walker was going to forgive me for losing the money. Instead, he said, "No, you're the one who was stupid. Anyone who could get conned that easily needs to pay the bill." So he took it out

1949 | Baron Walker and Bob, Pleasantville, NJ (corner of Lake Place and Main Street)

of my salary, which was nearly all of my weekly pay, but my manhood was called up, and that was much needed from living with my mother and five sisters.

I worked with Baron Walker for five years and during that time he would leave on various business and family trips. When he was away, it was up to me to run the business—planning, banking, accounting, opening, and closing. He would come back days later and find everything in perfect order. To find out whether I was honest or not, he would turn the clock in the cigarette machine to 7 am, the time I was supposed to open. Then he would ask me what time I opened that morning. I would tell him and he would check the clock hidden in the machine. I didn't know it, but when I came in and turned on the lights, the clock would start, revealing my opening time. His leaving the whole place in my care and making me accountable brought me out of the teen-age crazies into maturity and some degree of manliness.

Lessons in Providence

In 1945, Japan surrendered and I felt both joy and disappointment because my whole life was geared to enter the Navy and I thought I had missed my opportunity. But in 1950, we entered the Korean War and the Navy was seeking volunteers, so I went in to join. I was about to turn 20 years old and had this deep gut feeling that I should go in and enlist on my birthday, which was December 29, rather than wait until the first of the year. It was a strong impression that I didn't recognize at the time as the Lord. I went against a lot of family voices but enlisted on my birthday.

My timing really was of the Lord because after the first of the year hundreds

1950 | Bob in Navy uniform

of men joined, and they didn't have enough clothes, boots, space in training classes, barracks, or food for them all; the whole thing was a logistical nightmare and many men went without essential items. I got in just ahead of that, signed up for four years as Pharmacist's Mate and had everything I needed supplied to me. My service number was 4382355 and my basic training was 20 February 1951 in Great Lakes, Illinois where temperatures averaged 20 below zero.

I loved the Navy so much they used to call me Gomer Pyle. Everyone, including the Chief Petty Officer, could tell where Bob Mumford was because I walked like a duck and wore my hair like the Fonz, combed in the back in an LA (a lamb's behind, not a duck's behind), and it was all curly and wavy.

One day we were coming back from boot camp and I saw that someone had put my mattress in the doorway so that everyone had to walk over it with their muddy boots to get into the barrack. There was no possibility of getting a new mattress, so I turned it up on the cleaner side and slept on it that night. But, boy, did I have a time getting that thing clean and ready for inspection the next day!

After basic training, I was transferred as a Navy hospital corpsman to Bainbridge, Maryland at the U.S. Hospital Corp just outside of Dover, Delaware. The guys were all between the ages of 19 and 21; I was going on 21 so was one of the older ones. I was in the very first class, and for me, it was an unbelievable

Bob →

Lt. Clutter

U.S. NAVAL HOSPITAL CORPS SCHOOL
BAINBRIDGE, MARYLAND
25 AUGUST 1951
CLASS 1 - 51

1951 | US Navy Hospital Corp, Bainbridge, MD

amount of fun. I had always wanted to be a doctor, and this was as near as I could get. I loved it and excelled in everything. I was stationed in Bainbridge for six months and because it was a first-year class, we had advantages that the other classes didn't like additional instructors, training materials, etc. We were trained in lab, basic surgery, first aid, and first responder.

After Bainbridge, I was assigned special duty at the U.S. Naval Hospital in Philadelphia. A nurse by the name of Lt. Clutter worked it out so that I could stay near my sisters and go home every weekend as I was still the surrogate father of the family. Since most of my financial needs were met playing poker on the weekends, I sent every paycheck from the Navy to my Mom to take care of the family.

At the hospital, they had a big push to take all the Navy corpsman out of the hospital and send them to the Marine Corp. Lt. Clutter scratched my name off that list and said, "This guy is not going into the Marines." Even then God's providence was working on my behalf.

A couple times Lt. Clutter guarded my life and future. On one occasion, I had a Navy Commander with cancer of the throat under my care. He was in the process of dying and we were about to have an inspection by an Admiral, the highest level of inspections. The Commander didn't like me, and I didn't especially like him, but he was my patient, so I took good care of him. I bathed and dressed this officer and had the sick bay in "ship shape"— everything was perfect by Navy standards. As soon as I turned around to the door to greet the Admiral, the Commander threw himself out of bed and onto the floor to spite me. When the Admiral saw him on the floor, I thought, *I am dead meat.* When no one was looking, the Commander looked at me from the floor with a cocky smile, and I knew he was being vindictive. Lt. Clutter said, "Admiral, I know this man (referring to me), and what you're seeing is not what it appears." I would have been court martialed had she not stood in the gap for me. She did something similar to this at least three different times.

While trying to figure out whether to go into orthopedics or go the psychological route, I considered volunteering in the psych ward because I love people. I got on an elevator with five psych ward patients and pushed the button to go up. The patient standing beside me said, "Moo, we are all cattle here, Moo." I wasn't sure what to expect in a psych ward, but this freaked me out! I went up to third floor, everyone got off, and I took the elevator back to the surgical floor. When I got off the elevator, Lt. Clutter said, "Well, welcome home." She must have known. After that, my choice was surgical, specifically ear, nose, and throat.

Preparation for Father's Purpose

Looking back, I can see that every event was from the hand of the Lord. I went from the hospital corps to the Navy hospital, to a commission as Pharmacist's Mate on the USS *Aludra* stationed in Norfolk. When I got there, I was a third class petty officer and had a chief petty officer named Varner who was in charge

USS Aludra

of the sick bay. I loved this man; he reminded me of Popeye. He was a confirmed alcoholic and within a few weeks he was confident that he could depend on me, so he hardly ever came to the sick bay. At times I didn't see him for 2 or 3 weeks. It forced me to figure things out on my own. That's when I realized what my mentor, Baron Walker, had done for me. Baron had trained me to run that gas station by myself, which also prepared me to run the sick bay by myself. Varner would come to me drunk and ask me to do the reports on a manual typewriter with four copies of carbon paper then say, "Don't fail me, Bob." So I taught myself to type. He'd say to me, "You don't know how important it is that the Lord sent me someone to carry this." At 21 years old, I didn't understand it, but he saw it clearly. He inadvertently served God's purpose in my life, like Eli creating a vacuum for Samuel.

As I mentioned, I quit school in ninth grade in order to care for my sisters. Since I did not have an opportunity to do so before, I finished my high school education while I was in the Navy. My leisure time was spent playing poker, preparing for the GED test, and perfecting my touch typing.

While stationed in San Francisco before I came back to the Lord, I would spend a lot of time in bars with my buddies. It has been said that alcohol is a kind of truth serum and that when someone is half drunk what lies dormant within begins to come out. On several occasions when I had had more than enough to drink, I would start telling the people in the bar that this was no way to live; *there must be a better way*. While in my backslidden state, I would then begin sharing about the love of Jesus, graphically describing how stupid the whole bar and alcohol scene was. They would all agree, nodding their heads, many with tears in their eyes. A heavy presence would come over everyone; the Holy Spirit powerfully convicted us all. My heart was speaking, however, I did not have sufficient knowledge to lead them to the Lord.

Our ship, the USS *Aludra*, under the command of Captain Morrow, carried a crew of 243 men. He was an unusually small man for an officer. The crew said when you get a small commander he is most often difficult because he has to prove his authority. The ship was real dungaree-navy, a freighter, refitted to be a 5-hold refrigerator with 6-gun mounts and equipped to travel by itself. The gun placements were 3-inch 70s and fired alternately. This is how I lost a significant amount of my hearing. We didn't know then to protect our ears; we only stuffed cotton in them, which did little. Our ship had all the equipment needed to keep fresh fruit, milk, and frozen meats and vegetables. The other ships were thrilled when we came because we were the supply ship, carrying necessary food. This was providential because when I came back to the Lord, His clear commission to me was to "feed My sheep."

In this picture, we were simultaneously providing supplies to the crews on both the destroyer and the

USS *Aludra* supplying an aircraft carrier
on the left and a destroyer on the right.

USS Enterprise, a huge aircraft carrier. We would hook up to the ships using cables to move the cases of supplies. On one occasion, a cable snapped hitting one of our crew in the face. They brought him to the sick bay and all I could do was stop the bleeding. I immediately transferred him to the carrier, which had three operating arenas. The medical officers on the carrier were amazed the cable did not take his head off.

Being a Pharmacist's Mate had many advantages, all of which I thoroughly enjoyed. Of my three closest friends, two were storekeepers and one was a cook. None of us had any money, so Everett Lamb (center) went down to his locker and sold all his fishing gear so we would have money to go ashore. My buddy to the left was Louis Voss and I am on the right. One was Polish and the other Italian. Louis was not in the picture, but he was the cook. The four of us formed

1952 | Bob and his Navy buddies

a kind of "inner ring" of the ship. So between us we had the run of the pharmacy, the galley, and all the stores on the ship. It was a perfect set up!

If we couldn't get the extra food or special privileges we wanted, we would identify the person in charge and I would call them up to the sick bay. I would hold his inoculation records out the porthole and say, "If I let this go, all your shots will be missing and you will have to get every one of them over again." It was half in fun and half-serious. Then they would nervously laugh and say, "What did you say you wanted, Gomer Pyle?"

I enjoyed the ship, thoroughly loved being at sea, and thrived in the demands of life aboard ship. I found real friendship, a manly sense of belonging, as well as a kind of security in knowing exactly what was required of me in military discipline.

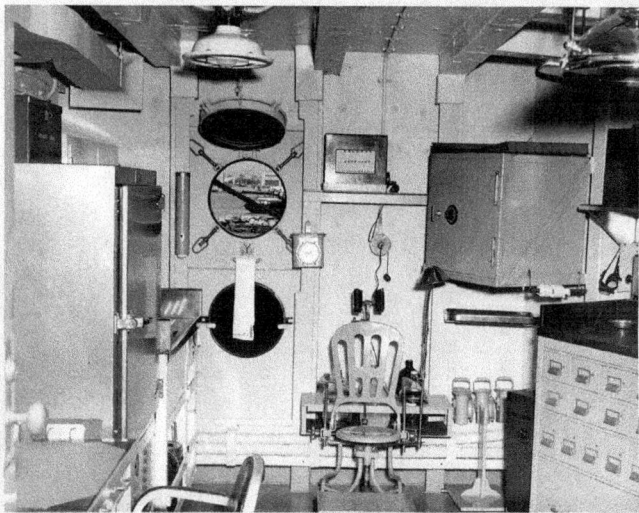

1952 | Bob's Sick Bay on the ship

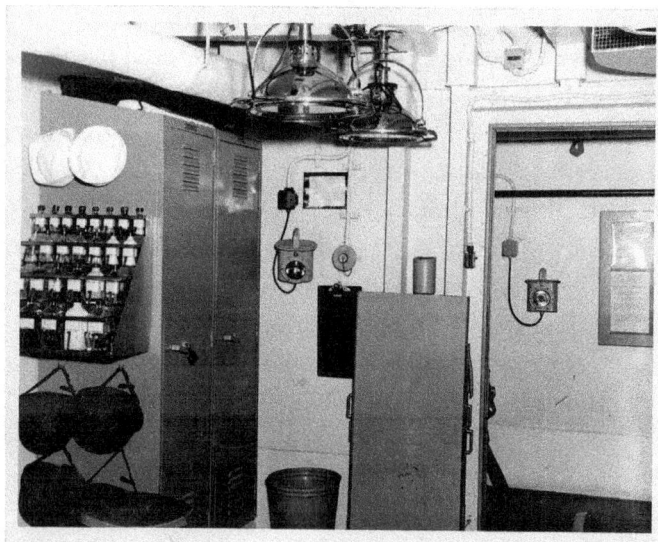

Louis, the ship's cook and I went ashore one day because he was eager to get a tattoo. I didn't want one, but he kept saying, "Just get an anchor." He got his tattoo first and passed out three times! When it was finally finished he said, "Okay, it's your turn," but I said, "No way!" When we returned to the ship, I had to dress his tattoo for four days to keep it from becoming infected.

By then, I was 3rd Class. We came back from commissioning the ship in Norfolk and went through the Panama Canal to berth in San Diego for the shakedown and crew training. The Navy trainers would drag targets for us to practice defensive accuracy. Eventually we learned to shoot them down. From San Diego, we traveled to Oakland Supply Depot where we replenished ammunition and loaded all the frozen food onto the ship before being deployed to Korea. In all, we made six trips between Korea and Oakland supplying the Navy ships.

The sick bay had two compartments. In the picture on the top left you can see the treatment chair and the safe in which I kept Old Grand-Dad whiskey— for medical reasons, of course! It was medicine for the patients and the bottles were marked and dated. Occasionally, I would transgress with the whiskey and pour a 4 oz. shot then put 4 oz. of distilled water back in the bottle and no one knew. But the whiskey got kind of light by the end of the bottle! The porthole is where I would threaten the crew with their shot records and below it is the blackout shield. I kept coffee and candy bars in my own fridge in the sick bay and would make coffee for my friends; we would drink three to five pound cans of coffee a week.

The other picture shows the operating table, surgical lights, and all medicine I used including morphine. I did a lot of removal of tattoos. On one occasion, I was treating a member of the crew and went out to get something. When I came back I discovered he had picked up the instrument pan and drank all the rubbing alcohol used for sterilizing. On the cabinet below the medicine is the battle gear and above it is where I hung my Navy hat. I always squared mine, which I thought gave it a kind of a salty look. Uncle Jack always squared his when he was on the destroyer.

The door into the sickbay was by the main passageway and when the ship was being supplied, I would reach out and take candy bars and coffee. Everyone knew I had fresh coffee, Heath bars, and Old Grand-Dad whiskey so I was quite popular with the crew!

Because I ran the sick bay, I basically had my own apartment with a 4-bed ward that everyone coveted. It had a medicine cabinet, my own sink and my own shower. They would say, "I don't believe you're only a 2nd Class hospital corpsman!" I didn't have to stand watches while everyone else had to stand four on and four off. I even had my own water cooler. When the ship was in lock down, no one could take a shower, but I could, because I had my own bathroom. And after sleeping in the attic or on the porch, this was pure luxury for me!

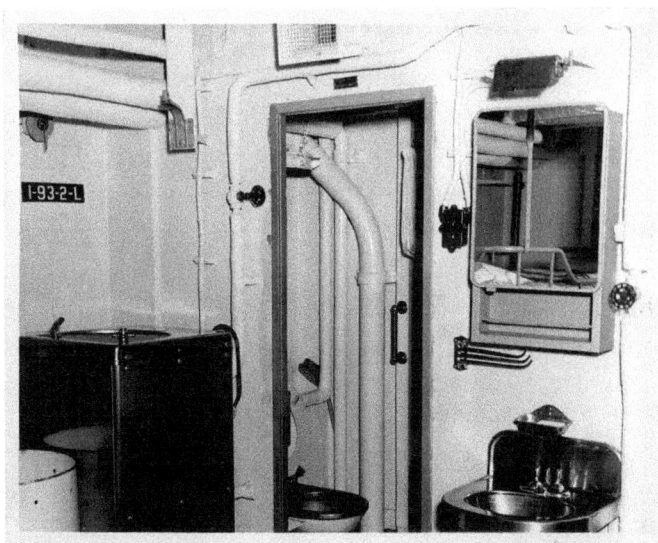

1952 | Bob's Sick Bay on the ship

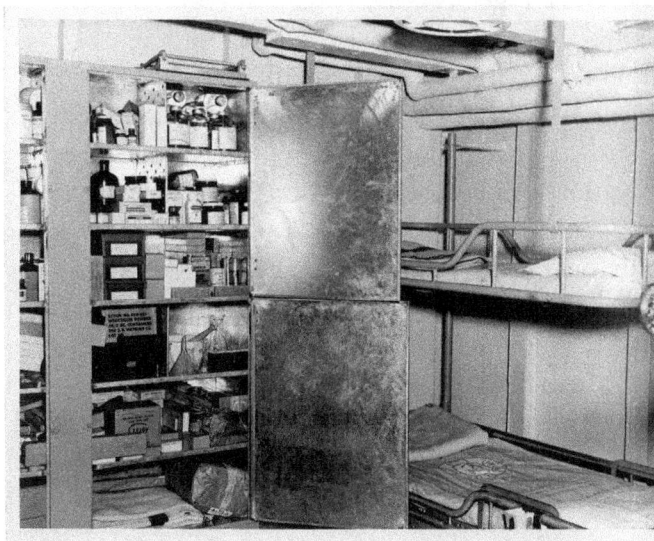

God's Call to Ministry

I developed meaningful relationships with the crew and knew them well. While I was stationed in Japan for a year and a half, my eldest sister, Diane, had an encounter with the Lord and was attending an Assemblies of God church in Atlantic City, New Jersey. She began writing to me about the Lord, which made me very defensive. Before I was to come home on leave, I called my sister and when I heard her voice, I knew something had happened to her. She said, "Bob, while you were gone I met the Lord!" I thought, "Oh great! Twenty-one days of leave shot!"

On March 16, 1954, I was home on leave and Diane pleaded with me to go to church with her. My conscience was so smitten because we had met the Lord together when we were younger and she had a profound influence over me. So, I agreed to go to church with her one time just to get her off my back. The pastor *happened* to be an ex-Navy man and I was wearing my uniform. He preached a very strong salvation message, seemingly directed at me alone.

Without an invitation, I went forward and was the only one at the altar. From behind me, I heard a cry like a woman in travail, and being a medic, I thought she was in labor ready to give birth. I turned around and saw a beautiful young African-American woman in intercessory prayer for me. She kept crying, "O God, have mercy! O God, have mercy!" As she travailed, I could literally feel the weight of sin and rebellion lift off me. I stood up, turned around, and said, "Well, I'm free!" Everyone rejoiced, especially Diane.

Many times I have wished that everyone could experience such a dramatic encounter as that. However, we need to be careful not to project our experiences on other people. For some people, forgiveness is a gradual process, while others have a dramatic encounter.

When I met the Lord, I smoked like a steam engine, two packs a day. The Lord, quite dramatically, reached deep down in me, releasing me from the desire to smoke. I wish He would have pulled out some other things like stubbornness and the need to be right as well, but I've had to walk through those over the past 60 years!

He also changed the way I talked. After my experience of commitment to the Lord, I literally didn't have a vocabulary with which to communicate. All the curse words I used were gone. And, I never said another bad word, neither was I tempted to slip. Perhaps He did that for me because those two things had such a hold on me, I don't think I would have gotten a fair start.

It seemed as if in a single moment I went from being out of God's will to being right in the center of God's will. However, I thought, if I'm going to be a Christian, I'm going to be the best one there is, so I swung from being very worldly to being very religious. Thus, I missed the mark and needed God's grace in a whole new way. Years later, I realized that this is where I learned about the third choice and the *Agape* road.

Before I met the Lord, I was clearly outside the borders of His grace. I thought I was a normal sailor—drinking, carousing, and presumably having a wonderful time. I was bumping the guardrail in worldly sin, but God's grace still kept me.

I was determined to excel, so I memorized Scripture until it was coming out of my ears and lost so much weight fasting that when I showered I had to keep moving to get wet! I stayed up all night praying, but no one taught me about the two kinds of sin. I didn't know there was such a thing as religious sin. I wanted to get so far from worldly sin that I went in the opposite direction and hit the other guardrail. When I came back to the Lord as a backslider I was determined that I was going to be His obedient servant. What I didn't realize was that knowing and understanding God comes by practice.

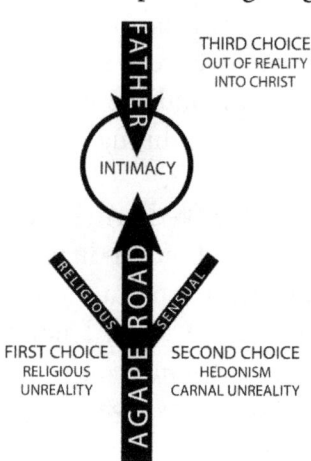

FATHER

THIRD CHOICE
OUT OF REALITY
INTO CHRIST

INTIMACY

RELIGIOUS   SENSUAL

AGAPE ROAD

FIRST CHOICE
RELIGIOUS
UNREALITY

SECOND CHOICE
HEDONISM
CARNAL UNREALITY

A few days after my encounter with the Lord, I was walking in town and passed a used furniture store. In the window was a great big family Bible. It was a New King James that had been well used, and probably weighed three pounds. I bought it and eagerly began reading.

Two weeks after my encounter with the Lord, I was back on the ship and was very nervous about witnessing to my friends and shipmates. When I returned, I found that every one of my close friends was on leave. God was giving me a chance to get oriented. They came back one at a time so I didn't have to witness to them all at once. When they saw me again, they could not understand what in the world had happened to me. During the three years prior to this, I had been such a hell raiser that my friends could hardly believe the transformation. When the guys would ask, "What happened to you?" all I could say was, "I saw the light." The entire ship's crew understood that Doc had "seen the light!" Then they'd ask, "What did you see?"

My two drinking buddies in the Navy were really close friends. The same day I encountered the Lord, both of those men were transferred to another ship. God knew that if those two buddies were free to influence me, I may not have made it. In ignorance I said, "God, why didn't You leave them here? I may have won them to You!"

When I came back to the ship, I began to read the four gospels, Matthew, Mark, Luke, and John, over and over. Someone had told me that the New Testament was originally written in Greek and I remember saying to the Lord, "I would like to be able to read the New Testament in Greek." Then I thought, what a dumb request, I haven't even graduated from the 9th grade!

I started a Bible study in the sick bay. About 25 guys attended twice a week. We would read Scripture and sing the words to hymns one of the guys would remember. One Sunday morning when I was only two months old in the Lord, the Chief Warrant Officer said to me, "Why don't you hold a service on Sunday morning in the ship's mess hall?" My first response was, "You've got to be kidding!" Within a few days the skipper granted permission and 40 or 50 guys who all knew me were in the chow hall waiting to hear what I had to say. I didn't have a very good reputation and they all knew about the dramatic transformation in my life. I talked to them right out of my gut and taught on Romans 8:1, "Therefore there is now no condemnation" and I still have the notes. Even though I hardly knew generations from revolutions, they were all thrilled with the Bible study. They really responded to this word of freedom because they knew my own history and sat there fascinated.

The Chief Warrant Officer turned to me and said, "Man, that was good stuff! Maybe you missed your call." When he said this, the Spirit of the Lord came on me and I was aware that there was even such a thing as a call of God and that there was one on my life. I knew that God had called me and it was incredible to me that the Lord could use *me* in this manner. I felt the grace and favor of the Lord as I explained to these men what God had done for me in my vodka drinking, "meaner-than-a-junk-yard-dog" state. This is how God called me to the ministry and I never looked back.

Within four months of my conversion, I was holding church services every week in the mess hall with 40 or 50 guys in attendance. The Catholics did not have a priest to hold a service for them, so they also joined us. I was not preaching; I was just sharing my story of how I met the Lord and how I met persecution. I would simply open the Scriptures, share, and pray for their families.

Many of us consider ourselves losers before God found us. I was from the other side of the tracks. My mother and father were divorced and I dropped out of school in the ninth grade. My life was a disaster. Yet Jesus saw that I had potential to find "THAT." I read Philippians 3:12, "Not that I have already obtained it or have already become perfect, but I press on so that I may lay hold of THAT for which also I was laid hold of by Christ Jesus" I knew I had found it. Jesus deals with us and works things out in our life, not by what we are, but by THAT which He intends us to be. It is very possible to be a believer in Jesus Christ and still miss God's purpose and plan for our life.

Because our ship was too small for a full-time chaplain, my well-known encounter with the Lord began to identify me as the unofficial chaplain of the ship during my last 10 months in the Navy. The officers would come to me and say, "You know that Thomas boy? Well, he needs you to talk to him." We never lost anybody due to bad behavior or an emotional blowout. And since the chaplain was also the mailman, I had three jobs—Doc, Chaplain, and Mailman—and enjoyed each role.

Even though I ran the sick bay, I wasn't allowed to actually diagnose anyone. After seeing each person in the clinic, I had to write "DU" meaning diagnosis undetermined on their record. With this I was authorized to get the mail and transfer patients over to the carrier for more extensive examination. One Navy surgeon said to me, "Mumford, you have some sort of intuitive gift of knowing what's wrong. You write DU, but each time you put me right on track as to what seems to be happening." My medical expertise was increasing, which really encouraged me, adding to the innate desire to become a doctor or a surgeon. The drawback was my insufficient education. I hadn't even graduated from High School.

Absorbing Human Failure

The men on the ship would often come to the sick bay at night because it was private—no one knew they came and no one knew they left. In a manner similar to Nicodemus, they would knock on the door at all hours of the night and say, "Doc, I have to talk to you." I slept most nights with my shoes on because I knew someone would be knocking on the sick bay door. I'd hear stories of people's lives and marriages disintegrating, one after another sobbing as they came to the Lord. I heard heavy stuff such as incest, sexual misconduct between client/doctor and parishioner/priest, all of which needed to be carefully guarded.

Eventually, word got out that they could trust "Doc," so the power of the listening ear increased and more and more men would come to me, opening their hearts regarding their baby who was seriously ill or their daughter who died, etc. All of them needed a listening ear and a person to care. They had come to believe that we were dealing with authentic Christianity.

In the following ten months, 29 of the crew members came to the Lord. These were very deep conversions, which were transforming for them and a joy to me. Others were putting in for transfer to another ship just to keep from surrendering to the Lord. They suddenly did not want to come to me for condoms or penicillin pills to prevent sexual diseases. The Chief Petty Officer became concerned and said, "Bob, you are going to have to figure out how to serve these men without embarrassing them."

One night the Chief Warrant Officer came saying he needed to talk. During the conversation, he came to the Lord and began attending the Sunday morning services. The sick bay was in his division of responsibility, so he began to engage quietly with all that was happening in the sick bay. We were mixing officer brass and white hats, which was very unusual.

On one occasion, I was standing behind a crew member who was drinking at the water fountain and I heard the Lord say, *Share the Lord with this man.* So, when he finished drinking I asked, quite directly,

"Do you know the Lord?" Suddenly, he blurted out, "Oh, no, my wife's prayers are being answered! Yes, I know the Lord and I don't want any of it!" When I said, "Yes, you do!" he started crying.

So my four-bed sick bay became the center of evangelism. Many came drunk, some sober, but all were broken and hurting. Out of such human agony, I learned about the garbage bag theory. People can't bear things alone; they have to unload on someone the strange and ugly happenings that anyone would prefer not to know. That was the beginning of the Kingdom concept of learning to absorb human failure.

The Lord's Voice in a Typhoon

I learned to hear the voice of the Lord. Once we came through a typhoon off the coast of Taiwan with 20 to 30 foot waves. The Lord said to me, "I want you to get in that bunk and rest." I remembered reading some Scripture about the sleep of the redeemed is peaceful, so while other crew-members were seasick and being thrown around the ship, I strapped myself in the bunk and slept through the whole storm! The porthole looked like a washing machine as we were doing 20 to 26 degree rolls. At one point, I looked outside through the hatch and there was an old fisherman's bamboo boat out there in the raging Typhoon. It was a small hibachi boat with two small fisherman, a woman and a man. I could not fathom how they were faring in the storm, but the boat appeared to be seaworthy, so I waved to them and they returned my greeting.

Ships would often rise up on the waves and then break in half, especially the C2 type hull, which the *Aludra* had. After that storm, we went back to dry dock in Oakland for refitting and found there were at least 38 rivets at mid-ship that had been sheared off from the pressure caused by the bow and stern coming out of the water due to the size of the waves. Everyone was shocked to realize that our ship had almost come apart.

One of the smaller aircraft carriers in dry dock was in need of serious repair because the bow had rolled back like a sardine can; the flight deck was peeled open and the lifeboats, which had been welded to the ship had been stripped away.

Weakness in Human Nature

Engaging the guys who came to the sick bay in the morning to get out of work had its own excitement. The officers were pleased with how I handled these situations. I would take an empty capsule, a good size one, usually size 9, and fill it with ACP, which is aspirin and charcoal mixed together until it was gray. This made an unusual but effective *placebo* pill. Then I would say to them, "You can't tell anyone I've given you this. If it makes you dizzy, don't take the second one, if it doesn't, take two." You should've heard the testimonies. They'd toss and sweat in bed but the next day they were completely "well!" Then they would come back and ask, "What did you put in there?" Most of these guys simply needed personal attention and someone to call their name.

I also became adept at removing tattoos. Some sailors were desperate to get rid of the more radical tattoos before they went home. Removing them had to be done in secret because it wasn't a sanctioned medical issue. While I was working on them, they were vulnerable and would talk about all sorts of things including revealing why they got the tattoo in the first place. Thus, removing tattoos became a way of gaining camaraderie with the guys.

Though my position on the ship was only 2nd Class, the godly influence and favor I had spread among the men. One time we were in the Pacific Ocean off Wake Island and it was my birthday. I was coming through the line in the mess hall and my friend, Louis, the ship's cook, put a cupcake on my tray with one lit candle in it. Everyone was moved and I thought they were all going to burst out singing, "Happy Birthday," but they didn't. It was a very meaningful experience for me because you get so lonely when you are away from family. The weakness of human nature unfolded to me like a clear and readable map through these events, and it was deeply rewarding.

A Medical or Spiritual Calling?

Eventually, I finished all my work for First Class Petty Officer, had all the commendations, and was signed up to transfer to nuclear submarine duty for another six years so that I could be on independent duty as the medic on the submarine. My desire and intent was to make a career out of the Navy and thought about seeking the position of technician for medical equipment repair. I thought it would be great to fly all over the world repairing U.S. Navy medical equipment that was malfunctioning.

However, due to the success of the Sunday morning services, one day I came back from rounds and the Chief Warrant Officer was waiting for me in the chair in the sick bay. He said to me, "If I have ever seen anybody who was called to the ministry, you are!" It seized the deepest part of my person and I was introduced to the thought of going into the ministry.

Since I loved the Navy so much, I decided not to transfer to a nuclear submarine when my tour of duty was over. Instead, I would get my college degree, obtain a commission, and return to the Navy as a career Chaplain. However, when I came home on leave, I realized I couldn't sign up because I needed to get my BA Degree before I could get my commission and become a Navy Chaplain. I was very motivated to finish my education because I could see the mission field! So, in my spare time I began my General Education Degree classes that I'd left when I dropped out of school in the 9th grade. Eventually, I finished my high school education and was soon qualified 1st Class and could sign up for college classes.

Aftermath of War

Meanwhile, our ship had been going back and forth to Korea. As a supply ship, we were part of a larger Navy flotilla. The Admiral in command, coming in on one of the ships, commented that if we mis-judge the massive 30-foot tide change, we would be dead in the water because the landing craft would be beached allowing an easy invasion.

The Korean War, like all wars, was ugly. We received many wounded men whom we were to transfer to Japan. Sometimes all I could do was give them pain relief or IVs of Sodium Pentothal allowing them to sleep and recover from the trauma.

During the Korean War, the conflict in Vietnam began to take form. Our ship was assigned to enter Vietnam five or six times prior to U.S. military activity. I remember the strength of the torrential rains there; we had to keep our faces down like in a shower or we couldn't breath. Although we were a supply ship, we were given the assignment go to a ship that had hit a mine with their minesweeper and retrieve the bodies. It was a brutal sight and made us grateful that our ship escaped any direct battle conditions.

When we were in Japan, we steamed into the Tokyo harbor and could still see the sunken ships in the harbor from the Second World War. The riggings and scopes of sunken ships and submarines stuck up out of the water in the harbor. It was a strange feeling to be in Japan five or six years later and see that they still hadn't totally recovered. Every experience with the Japanese people was memorable and rewarding.

What became exceedingly clear to me was that the military as a system was very brutal, but the people as individuals were not. This was the seed to my understanding how systems rule and years later, I wrote the book *Dr. Frankenstein and World Systems*.

Discharge from the Navy

In 1954, my time for discharge was at hand. My duty ended in Sasebo, Japan and I awaited transfer back to the States on an LST along with 250 Marines and Navy sailors. An LST is a Landing Ship Tank that took 17 days to cross the ocean and you could hear every wave bashing against the square bow of and bottom of the ship. It was known for driving guys crazy by the time they arrived. My child-like prayer was *Lord, would You please help me not be assigned to an LST to go back to America?*

Everyone in the holding area was clearing out, except for me and one guy who was waiting for his dentures and couldn't go. They were put on three LST's and sent across to Hawaii and then onto America. In some miraculous manner, my orders consisted of a train to Tokyo and a non-stop flight to Hawaii. That night, as I rode in comfort by myself toward Tokyo, I thought, *this Christian thing really works!* I ended up having three days of free time in Hawaii, then flew to San Francisco and was discharged on Treasure Island before I boarded another plane to return home.

Two Life Labs

After my discharge, I took a job at the Atlantic City Hospital. The supervisors knew my training was equal to a position somewhere between a Physician Assistant and a Nurses Aid, so I was given a lot of unusual jobs. One night an elderly man was brought in whom we soon discovered was one of the wealthiest men in Margate, New Jersey. He had slipped in the tub, cracked his skull, and died at the hospital.

As I was preparing his body for the morgue, the bell rang, diverting my attention. An ambulance brought in an elderly, African-American man who lived on the city dump. I could see the layered callouses on his feet, revealing that he had gone barefoot most of his life. He was very tender and I said, "I'm not supposed to say this, but can I ask if you know the Lord?"

He smiled with tears in his eyes and said, "Yes!"

I asked, "Do you have any fear of death?"

He took a deep breath and responded, "No, it's time." I held his hand, read some Scripture, and comforted him until he died. Then, I prepared his body and placed it in the morgue right beside the wealthy man.

Suddenly, it hit me, this was like the parable of the rich man and Lazarus! In the mortuary their bodies were drawer to drawer, side by side with the same date on their toe tags. This life lab taught me that death was the great equalizer.

Entering my second year as a believer, I was an eager new Christian. One day I was speaking love words to the Lord and heard Him say, "Were you a medic in the Navy?"

"Yes, Lord, I was."

"I'd like for you to gather up all the instruments and medicines you collected from the Navy and return them."

I was stunned and thought I heard wrong, so I responded, "I rebuke you, devil!" Without question I knew I was on my way to the federal penitentiary at Leavenworth! But, the Lord was persistent and I was eager to properly respond to His request, so I gathered up all the equipment and supplies and put them in a brown paper shopping bag and drove to the U.S. Naval Air Station. I nervously walked up to the gate, but the officer didn't question anything and allowed me to walk right in. In the dispensary, the civilian employee assisted me in placing all of the articles back on the shelves and as I walked back out those gates, I literally felt joy and freedom. I remembered the Scripture, "He guides me in the paths of righteousness for His name's sake" (Ps. 23:3). In this life lab I learned that obedience is challenging, but it certainly has its rewards!

Entering Bible College

A few weeks after my discharge, I enrolled in Eastern Bible Institute (later the name changed to Valley Forge Christian College) to begin studying for the ministry. It was hard for me to make the shift, but the Lord seemed to press me toward other avenues of ministry rather than that of U.S. Navy Chaplain. During this time, the Lord said to me, *Your greatest reward will be a hungry audience.* I have lived to see that fulfilled many times over.

My first year, I was elected president of the missionary society at the Bible College and began to see a mission field bigger than the Navy. I could hardly contain it. I saw the nations of the world and the Navy looked like a rowboat in the ocean. I entered Bible College to become a Chaplain but soon saw that God had different plans for me.

I met Judith in September of 1955 at Eastern Bible Institute in Green Lane, Pennsylvania. She was the most beautiful woman I had ever seen. As soon as I saw her, I knew she was to be my future wife. Simultaneously, when she saw me, the Lord said to her, *There goes your husband.* It was love at first sight.

Before I met her, I was making straight A's. Within a few months, my grades dropped to B's, then C's! I was smitten by the love bug and couldn't get my world together.

Judith was being romanced by another young man named Otto.

1954 | Judith Huxoll

I went to him and said, "I just got home from the Navy and I think she is my girl. If you think you are her boyfriend, you'd better get a good grip on her because I'm going to take her off of you." That was my big, bad Navy talk. I thought I might even have to fight him and if I did I would've kicked his butt!

So, I began to romance Judith. On our first walk down the lane I told her we needed to figure out how we were going to get married. She was shocked, but I never doubted or questioned that she was God's choice for me.

Expelled from Bible College

Eastern Bible Institute was rooted in holiness and some aspects of it were very legalistic such as the "six inch rule." Girls and boys could not be within six inches of each other let alone touch each other, not even to hold hands. Well, as a 24-year-old ex-sailor, I was convinced that the "six inch rule" was the dumbest thing I ever heard of. So, one night under the lamp post where couples said good night, I asked her if she would kiss me under the light where everyone could see. She said, "Yes," and I kissed her passionately! Part of the kiss was because I loved her, but in truth, the other part was a sense of defying the six inch rule.

That landed us in the hot seat. There followed a major legal procedure and an announcement that "Bob broke the rules, but it was not sexual." I was glad people didn't get the wrong impression. Judith was able to stay in school, but I was expelled for the rest of that term and I went back to Atlantic City to work for Baron Walker for the rest of that year.

Ask, Seek and Knock in the Oil Room

When I was working for Baron at the gas station during those months, I would go out, serve the customer and then run back into the oil room to seek the Lord. While I was waiting in the oil room, the Lord began to pour a message in me—point by point. I would run out to pump gas in another car and clean the windshield, then run back where the Lord would impart to me point two. As I was attending to the customers, I would pray in the Spirit, barely aware of what I was supposed to be doing. I had my big family Bible on top of a big stack of oil cans, and I would read, pray, write, and have my own personal camp meeting. A rather serious and complete outline for a talk came clear. I knew nothing about seeking and a little about knocking so I said to the Lord, "You have given me something that is burning in my soul and I'm knocking. Won't You open a door of opportunity for me?"

There are three ways to find and go through a door of opportunity.

First there is the intentional asking, "Lord, won't You give me the opportunity to share what You have done for me, revealed to me, and taught me?"

Then, there is the passive approach, "Well, if the Lord wants to open a door for me, He knows my name and address; He knows where I am." This could be why many Christians are still waiting for the Lord to open doors, often many years later.

Then there is the Mumford style—you tear the whole door off the hinges or pick the lock to get in! I have been in rooms and areas that didn't belong to me, sometimes at great personal expense. I didn't really understand about knocking so I often tore the door off the hinges and went in where angels fear to tread, saying, "Lord, if I survive this, I will tell others to be sure to knock!"

Knocking is a bit easier. "Lord, give me people to witness to today. Bring across my path someone who needs to hear what I have to say. Show me who, what, where, when, and how You want me to minister and open a door." When you knock and the Lord opens the door (from the inside), then you can step into that opportunity in confidence.

God never opens the door to situations we are too immature to handle, keeping us from getting in over our heads. Knocking has to do with sharing. There are opportunities waiting for each of us *if we knock*. If we don't knock at all, everything and everyone seems to become stale. If we tear the door off the hinges, we get into realms for which we are unprepared. We must learn the skill of knocking then learn to wait.

So, I had this message with three great points and I wanted to preach so bad I could hardly stand it. I said, "Lord, would I like to preach somewhere what You have given me!" A little while later, my Mother called and said, "Bob, one of the pastors here just called and wants you to preach for them Sunday morning." I said, "I don't care who it is or where it is, tell them I'll be there! Tell them I'll even pay them twenty-five dollars for the privilege!"

There are opportunities for everyone if you start knocking. It's a simple thing. However, don't knock before you have something to share. Ask and receive… seek and find…then knock and the door opens. I call this the *Law of the Father's Wisdom*. If you don't understand this, then all Christian service will be done with a human/soulish drive which disallows our survival on the long and treacherous journey. There are many Christian workers who begin with soulish desire and zeal. There are hundreds of casualties of Bible colleges and seminary graduates who are not in the ministry today because of failure to knock. If we knock, God opens the proper door of opportunity. Entering, we discover a large room full of new and exciting things. And when we have explored and examined all that's in that room, we see another door.

Breaking Condemnation and Guilt

During the time I was expelled from Bible College, my Mother taped a Scripture to the inside of my desk hoping to reduce some of the pain I felt for having messed up my life forever. The verse was, "My grace is sufficient for you, for power is perfected in weakness. Most gladly, therefore, I will rather boast about my weaknesses, so that the power of Christ may dwell in me" (2 Cor. 12:9). The Lord used that Scripture to break the condemnation and guilt I felt for being expelled from school for such a rash act. Many of the Bible characters are good examples for us in this because God chose to reveal their failures as well as their successes. God's grace became a theme for my life and teaching.

Missions Money in the Coke Machine

In Bible College, I had shared with Judith what I felt called to. I talked about my dreams of the Navy chaplaincy but said to her, "I think it's bigger than that—I am seeing a vision of the world and you're going to have to be committed to this and go with me and support me." We had no idea how big it really was. It was worldwide and she has been with me through it all!

1956 | Judith and Bob

Judith and I decided to head into the mission field. I remember saying to the president of the Bible College, "What is the possibility of our taking the Coke machine out of the school because the students are putting their mission's money into that machine!" Talk about commitment—every quarter and every dime counted!

Walter Beuttler, who was my teacher and spiritual mentor, said to me on graduation day, "If I were running this school, I would ask you to come back on staff in the fall." I was flattered!

While we were still in Bible College, I began a little mission church, functioning as the pastor as well as driving the Sunday school bus.

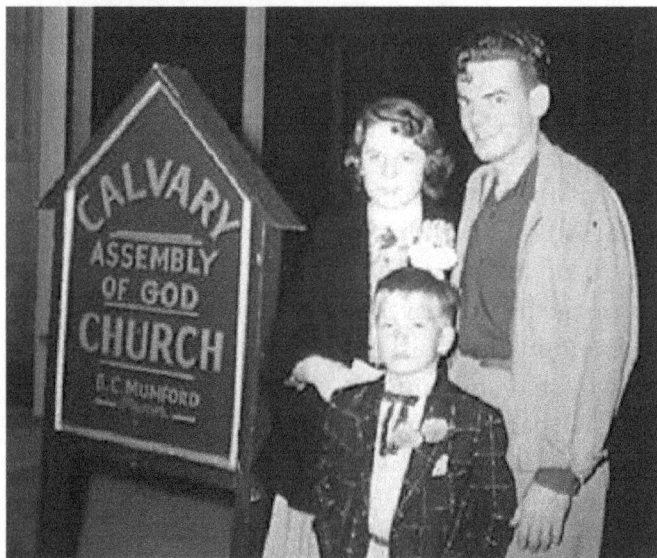

1956 | Judith Huxoll, Bob, and Judith's brother, Jim Huxoll

Wedding Bells

We talked about getting married when we walked on the lane and we agreed it was right. On summer break I traveled to Pottstown, Pennsylvania where Judith was visiting her family and asked her to marry me and move in with my family in Atlantic City. She shared a room with my two sisters, Janie and Joy for a few months before we were married on May 12, 1956.

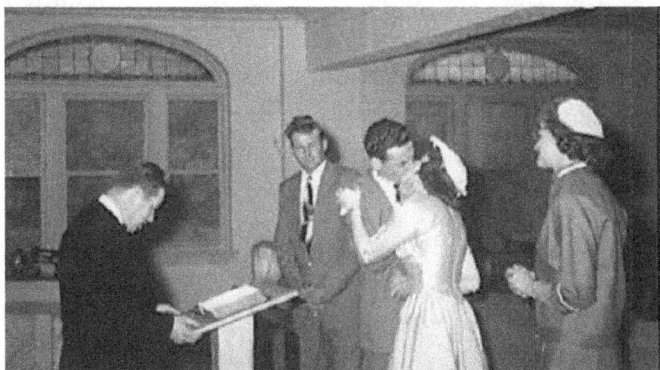

1956 | Wedding Day - Bob's sister Peg Wills and her husband George stood with us.

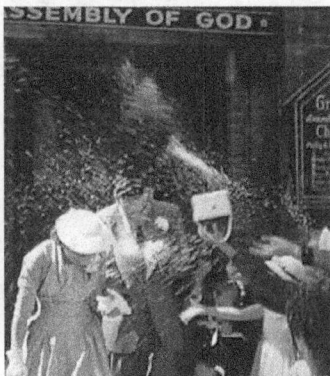

Our wedding was after the Sunday morning service at our home church in Atlantic City. After the service the pastor made an announcement inviting everyone to stay for our wedding. All of our family members were there, too. It was a warm and wonderful ceremony. For our honeymoon, we took a Greyhound bus to Miami, Florida to visit my father who gave us a small apartment to stay in for a few days.

The rules at Eastern Bible Institute required students to stay out of school for a year if they were married, so we lived with my family in Atlantic City during that time. Our first daughter, Keren, was born 10 months later and Beth, 15 months after that. In September of 1957, we returned to Eastern for my second term.

1957 | Bob and Keren

1958 | Beth and Keren with Judith and Bob

Summer on the Indian Reservation

Our first real assignment in Bible College in the summer of 1959 was to help the official missionary of an Indian reservation in Tonawanda, New York. We were missionaries there for three months to the six-tribe nation of which Mohawk, Blackfoot, Iroquois, and Cherokee were the main tribes. Several missionaries before us had mixed Christianity and the ceremonies of the Indian longhouse. Because of this, the longhouse had many Christian symbols as well as demonic ritualistic symbols all mixed together. It was a difficult assignment, but

1959 | Our mobile home before moving to the Indian Reservation

God's grace gave us some fruit that remained. This is where God put steel in our souls for the years of conflict and warfare that were yet ahead.

We lived in a mobile home and while we were there, Beth who was a few weeks old and Keren who was less than 18 months old, contracted whooping cough from the Indian children. They were so sick that we really thought they would both die. Keren was worse, but both of them would cough until they turned blue. Judith and I believed deeply in divine healing, and although we had taken them to a doctor, we were really trusting God for their healing. Judith was a real soldier nursing them back to health and by the grace of God, they both survived without any permanent damage.

Medical Mission Training

Just after my graduation from Eastern Bible Institute in 1959, we spent a year at the Bethesda Missionary Medical School in Toronto, Canada. We were trained in surgery, obstetrics, laboratory and dental procedures, and emergency medicine with the intent to be missionary medics in the jungles of Peru. Judith was nominated best nurse and I was nominated Class Valedictorian for the graduating class.

Children were not allowed at the institute, so we had to leave Beth (age 1) with my mother and Keren

1959 | Judith holding Beth and Bob holding Keren; Beth and Keren with Bob's sister, Diane Fox and Mom, Margaret Foster

1959 | Judith and Bob at the Medical Missionary Training Institute in Toronto, Canada

(age 2) with my sister, Diane, in Atlantic City for a year. It was a very difficult time of separation from our two girls, especially for Judith, but we felt this was the key to future ministry as missionaries.

At the missionary medical school, there was a surgeon named Dr. Horsley who looked like Walter Cronkite. We called him Dr. Cronkite and he always asked for me to scrub in for surgical procedure with him causing some jealousy among my peers. I had some kind of insight and coordination in surgery. I could anticipate his next move and snap the necessary instrument into his hand, partly because I knew how I would want it done. He would smile and say, "Its instinct."

One of the surgeries with Dr. Horsley was very memorable. A 38-year-old woman with three children had pancreatic cancer. We scrubbed for surgery and put our masks on and then Dr. Horsley made the initial incision. Upon opening her up, we saw a cancerous growth the size of a large grapefruit. I looked at him and he looked at me, and he said to me, "You know, don't you?" I said, "I do." It was surgically impossible to excise that tumor without killing her, so he said, "Let's sew her up." We both had tears in our eyes as he put the organs back together and finished the closing sutures. He and I both faced the reality that surgery has its limits.

Her husband and children came in to see her, and within about ten days, she died. The hurt and pain of human suffering was so intense I began to understand why doctors harden and become professional.

Soul Doctor or Physical Doctor?

One night after a number of surgeries, Dr. Horsley asked to take me home. He said, "I don't have a son, and you are a natural surgeon. Perhaps you should consider surgery as your calling in life. If you will embrace this and stay faithful to it, I'll pay for all your college and pre-med expenses, and cover your costs through two years of internship and into residency." He sat there writing it all out in the steam on the window of his car—he offered to pay eight years of my expenses and said he would see that I got into the medical school of my choice. Then he said, "I'll give you three days to make your decision." I was ecstatic!

When Judith got home from working her night shift at the hospital, I said, "I think I've just been introduced to our future!"

I went into our bedroom in our basement apartment and began to pray about it and heard the Lord say, *No, I called you to be a soul doctor not a physical doctor and the souls of My people need to be healed more desperately than their physical bodies do.*

I went back to Dr. Horsley two days later and told him I couldn't do it. He said, "You are out of your mind!" It broke his heart because he was committing something like $200,000 at the time. But I knew I was being called to a different mission field.

I never regretted not becoming a surgeon even though I loved the medical world. Once I embraced the soul doctor calling, I was highly motivated and never wished I would have done it differently.

Expelled from AG Ordination

We came home from medical missionary school in Canada I was ordained by the Assemblies of God (AG) to go to the mission field. They had commissioned us as missionaries before we even went to do the medical training. While waiting to complete all requirements for the mission field before we were to be sent abroad, the AG gave me official permission to teach in a small, independent Bible School.

Without my knowledge, students began leaving Eastern Bible Institute, asking for entrance into this small school. The Assemblies of God became threatened because of political interests. Financial issues motivated them to ask me to leave the school. My posture was simple, "I can't do that. You gave me permission to teach here, and by reason of personal integrity I can't leave."

The next thing I knew, I was no longer ordained with the Assemblies of God! The only reason anyone was dropped from ordination with the denomination was due to sexual misconduct or doctrinal issues and they were well aware of what they were doing. I went to see the board—all 16 of them—many with their heads in their hands knowing I was being railroaded. I reminded them that they had given me permission to become an instructor in that small school. When I asked, "Do you realize what you are doing to me? Everyone will assume I'm a heretic or sexually promiscuous" one of the elders got up and left—he couldn't handle the politics.

It took me a while to get over being expelled from the denomination, but God used this experience in very sovereign way because back then I thought the Assemblies of God and the Kingdom of God were synonymous. It took a while, but eventually I had absolute confidence that all that had occurred was ordered by a sovereign God. I began to see the Kingdom of God in a cosmic way.

Cultivating Compassion

While I was traveling as an evangelist, Judith and I moved to Kane, Pennsylvania in 1961 where we stayed for one year to pastor a church. There we almost lost our daughters for the second time.

The church property was next door and we were in the midst of construction of a new church building.

1961 | Bob praying and teaching Keren and Beth to be grateful before opening Christmas presents

The men in the church had dug the foundation and it had rained for several days so we had to wait for dry weather to continue construction. I was away on a ministry trip and in the meantime, Judith had come down with the mumps and was bedridden.

One day during that time our two girls, Keren and Beth, were outside playing and fell into the muddy foundation. They called for help but were too far away for Judith to hear them. They began to sink further and further into the mud. By God's providence, one of the women from the church was coming over to check on Judith and bring dinner when she heard the girls crying. They had sunk to chin level in the mud and were screaming. The more they struggled, the deeper they sank. When the woman pulled them out, their clothes and shoes were sucked off them. Had the woman come even a few minutes later, we would have lost both of our daughters in a most gruesome manner. God is faithful!

In every family, church, business, or organization God gives us at least two or three of His unusual people to practice on. Don't laugh; you may be the one who others have to practice on! Judith and I had one older woman in the church who every time I started preaching would begin to speak aloud using the same memorized words. I tried everything to correct the situation. I tried talking and getting her delivered; I counseled her and even offered to help find her another church. Nothing worked. There she was on the front row determined to interrupt every single Sunday.

This happened so often that one day I came home and our two daughters had their dolls lined up on the sofa. They were having a pretend deliverance service casting demons out of their dolls and they were using the same words that this woman used. I was appalled that they had actually memorized it! Not knowing any better, I kept trying to correct this woman or move her out of my life and sphere rather than simply learning to represent God's nature of compassion by loving her with God's *Agape*.

Another lesson of compassion was even more painful. Spending time outdoors and deer hunting were some of my favorite activities. However, having cold feet was almost a plague. I literally saved and scraped for a year until I had sufficient funds to buy a pair of insulated hunting boots from L.L. Bean. I was thrilled when I opened the box; I was not quite idolatrous, but close. They were insulated to zero degrees. I put them on and walked up and down the living room in these brand new hunting boots like a little boy on Christmas morning.

The next day, my pastoral visit was to a man in my church who worked in a chicken yard. Winter in Pennsylvania brings in subzero weather and I saw that he was walking around all the chicken mess in his sneakers and I became angry. Before the Lord spoke, I knew what He was going to say. Inside, I was rebelling: "I won't do it! No, Sir! Let him freeze!" I just want you to know how a mature Christian pastor responds when asked to obey.

The Lord said, "When you are finished rebelling, give the man your boots!"

Day and night for the next day the Lord kept urging me to give him the boots and finally the voice of the Lord withdrew, but I knew what I was being required to do. Finally, with a mixture of joy and reluctance, I got the boots down from the shelf, kissed them goodbye, and drove over to the man's farm. I handed them to him and said, "Here's the boots, I hope you enjoy them. They are a gift from God, the Father!"

God chose to use the boots to teach me several things. He saw me turning in on myself and gave me the word to break out. Was I forced to give the man the boots? No. But when I obeyed Him, amazing things happened. As I walked away from the man, I was still angry, but by the time I got back to the car, I began to experience the joy of the Lord. I had been set free from myself and taught how to respond unselfishly in compassion! If I had known this was the end result, I'd have given the man the boots much sooner.

Learning to be a Father-pleaser

In 1962, we moved from pastoring in Kane, Pennsylvania to Conneaut Lake, Pennsylvania where I was commissioned to start a three-month Bible school. Provided for us was an empty furniture factory with many rooms and apartments to house the students and their families. It was equipped with a large kitchen, dining area, and showroom, which became my classroom. I was passionate about teaching the Bible and feeding God's people and He brought many students to the school. Together we learned to expound deeply on the Word of God, our hearts ignited to follow Jesus as true Father-pleasers.

1962 | Keren and Beth holding Bernard, 2 days old

Judith became the cook with the help of two supportive friends who came with us from Kane. We were on a slim budget and Judith purchased all the groceries, visiting the farms for eggs and produce. We were stretching the dollar, searching for nourishing, fresh fruits and vegetables. Our girls, Keren (4 years old) and Beth (3 years old), went everywhere with their mother.

Judith was six months pregnant with Bernard when she began having pains. Overtired, along with the stress of responsibilities, her doctor instructed her to get in bed and rest until the pains subsided or she would risk losing the baby. When Judith's two friends took over the food shopping and the kitchen duties for her while she recovered, we were both very relieved. Bernard was born on March 16, 1962 in Meadeville, Pennsylvania, healthy and strong. Our girls were "in heaven" holding their little brother. The gift of family comes from the heart of Father Himself! March 16, 1954 was a significant date for me because it was the day I came back to the Lord.

Elim and the Nations

In 1963, I took a position as Professor of New Testament and Missions at Elim Bible Institute in New York. I was the Dean and was given a classroom with nine blackboards, several on each wall of the classroom. I thought I had died and gone to heaven! Besides teaching a full schedule at Elim, I was out almost every weekend ministering at other churches to enable us to

1963 | Alene Huxoll (Judith's Mom), Bob and Judith at Elim

survive financially. Our salary was $100 per month, plus food in the cafeteria, housing, and utilities. With three children, it was a very exciting time.

As Dean, I was required to explain the rules. I began listing all of the social rules, dating rules, dress rules, etc. for the new school year sequentially on the blackboard. Having been trained at Eastern Bible College I was like a drill sergeant. There were 21 "there shall *be no...*" rules. The students started calling me "Beno" that year because I had so many rules. There were about 40 students in the room and as I was reading off the rules, one of the students asked, "Mr. Mumford, how many rules do you have?"

I answered, "Twenty one."

He said, "Even God only had ten!"

All of us know how to get around the law. We know how to slip and slide. What God's people need is an understanding of the passive righteousness that allows the Kingdom to come changing our behavior from within, not from without.

These early years were some of the most difficult of times financially, physically, and spiritually, yet the lessons learned were invaluable. We read the stories of men like Joseph, Daniel, or Jeremiah in their preparation for ministry, forgetting that these are examples for those of us who were yet to come. Every man and woman whom God has used has similar stories of living through difficulties. My intent is to exercise caution that we do not just learn the story and end up missing the lesson. If you *want* to quit, God gives us every opportunity to do so. It was at this very point in our lives that we were aware that God had indeed tested and approved us to carry His truth and love to the larger body of Christ.

1963 | Keren, Judith, Bernard, Bob, and Beth
at Elim Bible Institute

While teaching at Elim Bible Institute, doors began to open with the Full Gospel Businessmen group allowing me to teach on the renewal in denominational churches. I remember teaching 37 seminars on the baptism on the Holy Spirit in two weeks throughout New England. I taught every night and sometimes three times a day in different places. The momentum was powerful, the circumstances sovereign, and the fruit increasingly visible.

There came an invitation for me to take part in a convention in Lima, Peru and my accommodations consisted of staying with a local family. As you know, poverty there is indescribable. When I walked into that humble home, there was a little table set like the Waldorf-Astoria and beside it was one chair. All kinds of foods had been heaped on that table and the family was standing around it. I said, "When are we going to eat?"

My host replied in broken English, "Oh, no, we don't eat. The man of God is here. Our joy is to serve him and give him our best." The reverent tone of his voice made me want to turn around to see if Elijah had come up behind me.

I asked, "What will you eat?"

"Oh, we don't eat while the man of God is here. We will eat whatever you leave."

So, with father, mother, and nine children lined up around the wall, I sat down and tried to eat. I almost choked and the food turned to paste in my mouth. Tears dripped onto the plate. All the while, they were

1967 | Bob, Judith, Keren, Beth, and Bernard

thanking God, worshiping the Lord, and saying, "O God, we thank You that You have honored our house and sent to us a man of God." Something began to break inside of me. They had received me into their home just as they would have received Jesus Himself.

In Caracas, Venezuela, I was on a bus during a communist revolt. Suddenly, a rebel mob ran into the streets with machine guns and engaged the bus directly ahead of us. Bullets were flying and without warning, they turned the bus over on its side. According to the news, almost everyone had been burned alive. I was in the bus some 200 yards behind it. Our bus driver saw what was happening and quickly turned down a side street. This experience gave me a tremendous subjective understanding of what it would be like to come to the end of my life. In that moment I thought, "Here I come, Lord" and was kind of comforted by the response within me. I didn't have a sense of panic or fear but I thought, "As you see the day approaching buy up the opportunity." I wanted to hear, see, feel, and be part of what God was doing as long as He allowed me to.

The two things that we are responsible to share with others are prayer and our own personal, authentic experiences. When you ask the Lord for bread, you will be amazed how He gives you the right kind of bread that is needed at that moment. Sometimes that bread comes in the form of our own experiences. What we have personally seen, heard, and handled we should not apologize for because it is the manner in which Father has been working in our life. The man with the reality of authentic experience is not at the mercy of the man with a theory. God will give bread to anyone who asks and Jesus is the One Who dispenses that bread according to the need of people.

Pastor or Teacher?

It was a very difficult decision, but in 1966 I left the classroom and my blackboards at Elim and we moved to Wilmington, Delaware so that I could obtain a Master's degree from the Reformed Episcopal Seminary in Philadelphia.

This education prepared me for an amazing acceptance among mainline denominations, especially the Roman Catholics. I can vividly remember the first Eucharist or communion service in which I participated in the Episcopal seminary. With my Pentecostal background, it did not seem possible that the Holy Spirit visited places like that and I was greatly surprised when the conscious presence of the Holy Spirit swept over my person, allowing me to experience God's love and care for the whole body of Christ. It was a transformational experience that altered the direction of my life and ministry.

Our son, Eric, was born in Wilmington, Delaware in 1968. In addition to having four children and going to seminary, I pastored a church there and taught a Bible study every Friday night in Princeton, New Jersey, which was one of the highlights of my week. It was a vibrant group that met in a home and grew into a thriving church that functioned effectively for some 30 years. More people met the Lord and found the reality of the Holy Spirit in those Friday night meetings than we were able to measure. The church in Wilmington grew from 40 to 430 members in less than a year. Later I realized that they were coming because of my teaching gift, not because I was a great pastor.

Just as I was graduating from seminary, I got a phone call asking me to come to Philadelphia to meet a pastor who was very ill. When I arrived, the pastor got up out of his sick bed and took me into the sanctuary of his church. It was a beautiful church building with stadium seats, blue carpeting, and an amazing audio system. And it had a blackboard on the stage. After he showed me the church he said, "I am very ill and I own the title to all this. It is mine to give. If you will come and commit to pastoring these people, I will give you this building, title and all." I just knew it was God because it had a blackboard behind the podium. Not many 27-year-old pastors have an opportunity like this and all I could think was, *Um, YES!*

One of the prisoners at San Quentin once asked, "Don't you get suspicious at anybody who builds a 5,000 seat auditorium with all the seats pointing at himself?" But all I could see then was the light blue rug and "Bob Mumford, Sr. Pastor" in neon lights on the billboard.

It had a hold on me and the conflict started. I wrestled with this for days and finally said, "Father, what do You want in this?"

Father said, "Be My guest."

I said, "But I want You."

"Well, if you want Me, then say 'No.'" I could have had it and my whole life would have been different. I didn't have the terms for it then, but that was an area of conflict for me and through it I learned a little more how to abide on the Agape Road rather than choose an alternate road. I learned to hold on to THAT for me.

THAT

Philippians 3:12, "Not that I have already obtained it, or have already become perfect, but I press on in order that I may lay hold of THAT for which also I was laid hold of by Christ Jesus." The phrase "become perfect" is *telios* in Greek signifying arriving at the original purpose for which we were created. The word THAT is carefully circled in my Bible.

A small child, sitting at the dining room table drawing and his mother asked, "What are you drawing?"

"I am drawing God" was his prompt reply!

His mother quipped, "But no one has ever seen God."

He said, "Well, they will when I'm finished." THAT is what is in God's mind for all of us individually and corporately.

When Judith and I saw THAT, it transformed our entire approach to both ministry and life. Is it possible to see the difference between reaching for success and reaching for THAT. Like Paul, we can cease being motivated by success and engage all that it means to become a Father-pleaser; moving toward all that He had in His thinking for us in eternity. THAT, of course, is different for every person.

In my early Christian walk, I thought THAT for me was to be a *missionary*. I nearly put myself on the mission field by human strength when I was ordained in the Assemblies of God. I already had my missionary appointment to Peru and was making plans with our team when it all fell apart. So, I decided THAT for me was to be an *evangelist*. This implied that my responsibility was to travel and proclaim as an evangelist.

On one occasion, I was standing on the platform doing what I thought was the will of God. Six or eight people had come forward to receive Christ and I was preparing to pray for them when God said clearly and in a fatherly voice, "I didn't call you to be an evangelist."

I said, "What a time to tell me, Lord! I've got all these people standing here waiting, what am I going to do with them?"

The Lord said, "Just minister to them."

Afterwards I went home and said, "What do You want from me?"

The response was immediate and clear: "I called you to teach." Do you know how I know I am a teacher? I know it because God gives me the content to teach. My wife said, "People would be surprised if they knew how easily these things come to you." I sit quiet in the morning with my Bible and the Lord simply says, "Have you ever seen how Numbers 12 relates to 1st Corinthians?"

"No, I never saw that! Oh, look at that. Praise God." This is THAT for me—I found it!

When each of us commits to THAT, our entire world may be in for an unexpected transformation. Releasing us from human strength, altering and re-adjusting our self-made plans, we begin to enter the rest of which Christ has promised. Failure to discover our THAT, may be the reason for so much burnout.

When I found THAT for me was being a teacher, I was still a pastor in Wilmington and knew my strong teaching gift would quickly burn my congregation out. The passion to see everybody find the Kingdom was strong and expectant, because THAT was working in me.

One time I taught on water baptism and had five or six people signed up to be baptized after the service. When I was done teaching, I began the water baptisms, looked up and there were 25 people in the line. Those baptisms were so powerful that people were going home for a change of clothes and coming back with their friends and neighbors! I baptized people for six hours and can't even remember how many were actually baptized. Back then I was baptizing because it was biblical; now, I know the importance of baptism in changing governments.

For more than 60 years, I have enjoyed seeking to fulfill THAT. I would rather teach than eat because I found THAT. God will move heaven and earth to bring THAT into being in our life. Discovering it is like an abundant entrance into the Kingdom that has been given to us and our joy, purpose, and personal freedom flourishes. When we have personal freedom, we become more willing to impart freedom to others. When we have purpose, we are increasingly capable of imparting purpose to others.

Charismatic Renewal

Beginning in 1965, we participated in the outpouring of the Holy Spirit identified as the Charismatic Renewal. We found unusual favor and acceptance among the Catholics at Duquesne University in Pittsburgh. This, of course, was the direct result of the teaching gift being released. On one occasion I was asked to speak at a Catholic convent and remember going down three flights of stairs into the basement where 30 nuns and 20 novices were gathered. They wanted me to teach them about worship and the Person of the Holy Spirit. When I started to tell them about worship, the presence of the Holy Spirit swept the room and to my knowledge, nearly all of them received an exciting baptism in the Holy Spirit. That began a working relationship that

1969 | Mumford Family in CA

opened an entirely new sphere of God's goodness as well as new insights into Catholic spirituality to me. I discovered that many of Father's choice believers are called to function within the institutional framework.

From Delaware we moved to Southern California in 1969 to work with Ralph Mahoney and World MAP: Missionary Assistance Plan. Our mission was the cultivation and development of spiritual leadership and missionary training for third world pastors. We were holding six camp meetings a year up and down the California coast. We also developed a Bible class at Melodyland Christian Center's School of Theology under the leadership of Dr. J. Rodman Williams, who was part of Ralph Wilkerson's church. The Bible class consisted of 600 to 700 people every Friday night. Everyone from the Jesus People to high church Catholics all flowing together was a truly sovereign experience. I also

1969 | Jesus Movement - preaching and baptism with Lonnie Frisbee at Corona del Mar, CA

had the rewarding opportunity to contribute to what became known as the *Jesus Movement*. We had oceanside services and when asked if anyone wanted to be baptized, the Holy Spirit swept over the crowd and they came down in droves.

When I traveled I would take one of our children with me when possible. Even though they missed school, Judith and I felt the experience would broaden their world, exposed them to biblical principles, and give us teaching moments with them. On one fatherly

1970 | Bernard

occasion, I said to our eight-year-old son, Bernard, "Did you tithe your allowance?"

He said, "Why should I do that?"

"Because if you tithe your money, the Lord will honor you."

He looked at me with the 50 cents in his hand as he considered giving a tithe of it, which was a whole nickel. This was high finance to an eight-year-old and he said, "Did you try it?"

1970 | Bernard & Eric

I could have said, "No, but I read about a man who…." He wanted to know whether that tithe had any connection with the blessing of God. I said, "Yes, it does. If you will tithe, God will bless you, I have tried it. That's Daddy's experience."

My wife told me that at the service the next night he had about $1 in change and when the plate came by he dumped it all in. Judith asked him, "Why did you do that?" and he replied, "Because I need more money." Then we had to deal with motives and attitudes!

Beginning in 1971, we became officially involved with New Wine Magazine and Christian Growth Ministries and relocated our family to Ft. Lauderdale, Florida. Five of us teachers began

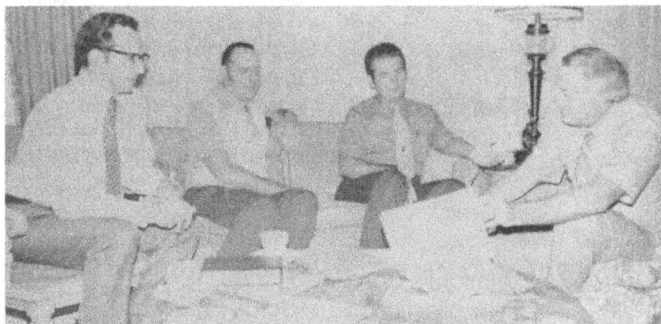

1971 | Charles, Derek, Bob, Don (Ern not shown)

ministering together: Derek Prince (Assemblies of God), Don Basham (Disciples of Christ), Ern Baxter (Charismatic), Charles Simpson (Southern Baptist), and myself, (Assemblies of God and Episcopal). There was a sense that between the five of us there would be a diversification of teaching that would give more balance and less emphasis on personality. Little did we know where all of this would lead us. The five of us were, indeed, naïve regarding the significance surrounding our initial commitment. Although we were all very different in personality, ministry style, and background, God gave us a unity born of the Holy Spirit. Three of the five of these anointed leaders—Don Basham, Ern Baxter, and Derek Prince—have since gone to their eternal reward.

In 1972, we began extensive seminars in many U.S. cities as well as many nations of the world. New Wine Magazine was carrying urgent nourishment for those who were seeking deeper spiritual truths. We sought to emphasize the truths of God's Word as we saw them emerging out of the strong out-pouring of the Holy Spirit. Our themes most often centered on spiritual unity, spiritual authority, more personal pastoral care, covenantal understanding, and discipleship. Basically, our vision sought to establish the truth needed to prevent the Charismatic Renewal from disintegration, corruption, or a religious type of degeneration into subjectivism and experience fixation. The response to these truths was remarkable.

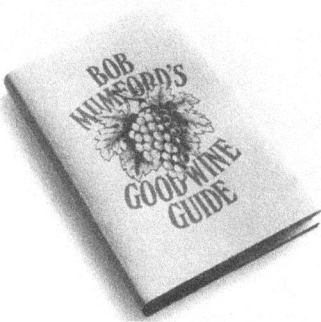

1972 | Bob Mumford's Good Wine Guide—a collection of New Wine Magazine articles about deeper spiritual truths

About this same time, similar truths were coming to America from the widely known spiritual visitation in Argentina. The clear cry was the need to harness the power of God to the wagon of God's purpose in world evangelism—people. The need for discipline, respect for leadership, and covenantal cohesion was becoming more and more apparent. Out of this came what is now known as the "discipleship/shepherding" movement. Like every movement, it had its supporters, those who were blessed and strengthened, but it also had its detractors and those who were injured or disappointed.

For the next few years Judith and I traveled globally and inter-denominationally, ministering to churches

1978 | Bob and Judith with Pope John Paul II in Rome

1977 | Bob teaching "Hindrances to Holiness"
in the Kansas City Chiefs stadium

involved in the Charismatic Renewal with great zeal, vision, and with measurable results. He allowed us the high and holy calling of ministry in some 40 different denominations and in more than 50 countries of the world. We had the unique opportunity to meet Pope John Paul II in Rome.

Large meetings began to emerge due to the cohesion and purpose of covenant relationships. The first conference of Lutheran/Catholics that I spoke at was held in Minneapolis/St. Paul with more than 12,000 Lutherans and Catholics worshiping together in one auditorium. It was history in the making.

All of this was consummated in 1977 in what became known historically as the Kansas City Conference. More than 55,000 people from 30 different denominations were worshiping God in Spirit and in truth. These were people who loved the same Jesus and served the same God, the Father of our Lord Jesus. Once we really *see* the larger body of Christ, Father seems to be more willing to give us access to it.

If there is one critical need in the Church today, it is for leaders who can *see* more than their own church, denomination, or agenda. Smallness of vision prevents God from sweeping over a city or moving powerfully in a given nation. I challenge our present leaders and ones yet to emerge to *pray that God would allow us to see His Church as He sees it.* If He grants us an answer to that prayer, He will also instruct the pastor or doorkeeper to open the door to the larger sheepfold. He opens it to us because we know how to *behave* ourselves when among those who worship differently. He knows we are trustworthy, respectful, and that we will not injure nor take advantage of those to whom He gives us access.

There is no question that God's presence is stronger and more powerful when denominations and other streams of influence embrace one another. After all, a denomination, any denomination is *an incomplete expression of the God whom we serve.* My THAT was to "feed My people." I could only do that after God purified my motives, purged my prejudices, and trusted me with access to His larger Church.

The closest I ever felt to God was standing on the platform at Kansas City when I said, "I've already looked in the back of the book and Jesus wins!" The power of God fell, surging through my physical body. The coursing of the Holy Spirit through my person was so strong that I thought I had been electrocuted and remember thinking, *My nerves will not hold this, I'm going to die! This is it!* The huge crowd began to worship and rejoice in a manner that would have to be experienced to be understood! The closest I ever felt to God was in the presence of more than 30 denominations or expressions of the great God we serve.

I Need Jesus

One of the surest ways to spare ourselves much of the painful dealings of God is to learn that little word *dependence*. I need Jesus. I am not playing games when I say that. I *need* Him. When God stops, I stop. If He does not have anything to say, that makes two of us.

Father allowed me to understand how this works in some meetings in New England where the teaching had gone on for a week and was progressively glorious. God was showing up, the place was packed to the doors every night, and people were getting blessed and healed. The final evening service arrived and I was to speak. I carefully sought the Lord all afternoon. I prayed and fasted, but nothing came. *Not to worry*, I said to myself, *the Lord has done this before. He will give me something to say during the worship service.* The worship was over and nothing happened. During the offering I started to go through my Bible to warm up some leftovers but nothing would come alive. The whole Bible was dry and the pages just stared back at me, refusing to speak. Finally, they introduced me and as I walked up to the pulpit I thought, *the Lord will give direction, He's waited this long before.* But I just stood there, a complete blank. Here it was, the final night of a significant week and the teacher comes to the pulpit with absolutely nothing to say!

The pastor was sitting down in a pew and I said to him, "Pastor, what shall I do?" He said, "I don't know." So I turned my eyes from him and looked over the congregation and as I did he jumped up from his seat and began to prophesy, "You have seen an object lesson tonight. It is not a question of man running or man willing but of God Who shows mercy." I became the object lesson.

After the prophecy I waited. Sill nothing came to my mind. There was a woman sitting toward the back with a large black hat. She looked very chic. I looked at her and the Lord said, *Ask that lady to play the piano.* I had no idea if she could even play but I looked at her and asked, "Lady, back there with the black hat, would you play something on the piano for us, please?" She looked at me, took off her big hat and came walking up the aisle. It was so quiet that you could hear people breathing.

She sat down at the piano and as she touched the keys, the presence of God filled the auditorium. It was beautiful! It turned out that she was a Christian who had fallen away and her own spiritual Father reclaimed her that night as she sat at the piano playing. Without explanation, the audience seemed aware of what was happening. I was still standing in the pulpit, essentially paralyzed, while everyone else was weeping. When the meeting was over I said, "Amen!" That was the total content of my contribution for the evening. A few years previously, I would have said, "God if You don't have anything to do or say, I'll just take care of this situation myself." But I learned to depend on Him.

Covenant Movement

In 1971, we moved to Ft. Lauderdale for the primary purpose of the development and maturity of new leaders. There was a fresh emphasis on discipleship rooted in a clear vision that we had for efficient and effective pastoral care. Words such as *fatherhood* came forcibly upon us as leaders, causing us to recognize that the Church was not designed to be a frustrated General Motors, but a family built relationally with spiritual fathers. Men like Luther, John Knox, and John Wesley were heroes of the faith. They functioned as spiritual fathers who led with strength and authority that was neither coercive nor dominating. Our intention in discipleship was to follow Jesus' model, attempting to train young men and women for leadership. The terms *mentor*, *disciple*, and *spiritual father* were all words that helped us understand that the Church was a family.

This family was essentially linear as well as vertical, and a hungry and confused Church quickly grasped the nature of commitment and covenant. However, as the movement grew, many people were injured in the initial unfolding of this truth because both leaders and followers walked with a degree of *immaturity* that was embarrassing. We saw ourselves in a military model, like commanders involved in spiritual warfare. And, as we all know, spiritual victories are not won without spiritual casualties. There is regret and grief over every mistake, and every idealistic application of a principle, grief over every young leader who was given authority and for whatever reason misused that authority whether to personal advantage or to personal failure. While I rejoiced in its great strengths, we also became increasingly conscious of its serious weaknesses. Every new visitation seems to move toward corruption, some took longer while others appeared to corrupt themselves with amazing velocity.

About 1978, the controversy on discipleship began. Personally, I found myself almost disillusioned. Only people who understand revival know the kind of problems that accompany a moving of the Holy Spirit on that scale. Some consolation was found in the fact that when God calls leaders, He has only sinners saved by His grace to choose from. God does not have mistake-proof options in His Kingdom; He, Himself proves that He is willing to risk. We began to understand how dangerous it was for Charismatic leaders to teach God's people what other pastoral leadership did not know. By doing this, we were contributing to the injury, pain, and pressure of a church and society that was already fragmenting.

While many of these original principles have been mastered and adjusted, I still believe in them with all my being. Presently, I am walking in the fruit and the joy of those specific principles and promises of God. Our desire is to share these with others in a real and effective way, since they have been purified by God's process of death and resurrection. The truth of covenant relationships is real and has been reabsorbed into the mainstream of the life of the Church. For that, I am pleased. However, there simply cannot be spiritual warfare of that magnitude and intensity without casualties. Like any military leader, we are forced to absorb human failure.

From Acorns to Oak Trees

The essence of failure as a leader cannot be measured numerically; it surrounds the fact of not knowing THAT. It also involves denying or refusing to give people under our influence the freedom to become an oak tree rather than remaining an acorn. Pastoring suggests that we are given "acorns" to cultivate and nourish until, they too, mature into oak trees, able to stand on their own feet and make decisions with integrity. When we deny people the chance to become strong and fruit-bearing oak trees, we exhibit tyranny and control. Control perpetuates the eternal childhood of the believer.

Our kids were learning some spiritual maturity. On one occasion I was laying on the couch with the flu. They came in and said, "Dad, the Lord told us to pray for you. So they prayed, "'God, in Jesus'

1978 | Bernard, Eric, Keren, Beth in Ft. Lauderdale, FL

name heal our Dad.' OK, Dad, get up." In faith, I staggered off the couch and almost threw up right on the spot! I did not want to deny them the opportunity for their little oak trees to grow some fruit.

It was also during these years that I learned that there is such a thing as having a *wrong* hold on our children. Fear and refusal to yield to the expectations of God the Father can have debilitating effects on both parents and children.

In January, 1972 I received a call at my office, "Your little boy is in the emergency room. He's been hit by a car." I met my wife at the hospital and saw Eric's distorted leg broken at the thigh and covered with blood. He was almost 4 years old and we were both in shock. The nurse excused herself to get something so Judith and I held hands over his little broken body and began to praise the Lord. The glory of the Lord's presence filled that room—we knew He was in

1972 | Eric celebrating his 4th birthday in traction in the hospital with Judith's Mom, Alene Huxoll (left) and laying on the sofa with Bob (right)

1973 | Bernard and Eric

control. Somehow we experienced an internal adjustment and were re-related to our children and free to love them in a different way. Eric was in traction for several weeks, then in a cast from the waist down with a bar across the middle to stabilize his legs. It was a long road to recovery for him, but he was very brave.

Eric had an unusual capacity for spiritual things. When he turned four years old, I asked him what he desired for his birthday. I thought he was going to say a bicycle or the latest toy. He looked at me and he said, "I want to be baptized in water with all my church there." So, we invited our little home group over and we baptized him in water. He came up speaking in a new language of the Holy Spirit.

A few years later, I had to learn about having a wrong hold on our children when our son, Bernard, came home one night and had been drinking. As I watched him walk from the car to the front door, weaving as he walked, I thought, "Good Lord, what

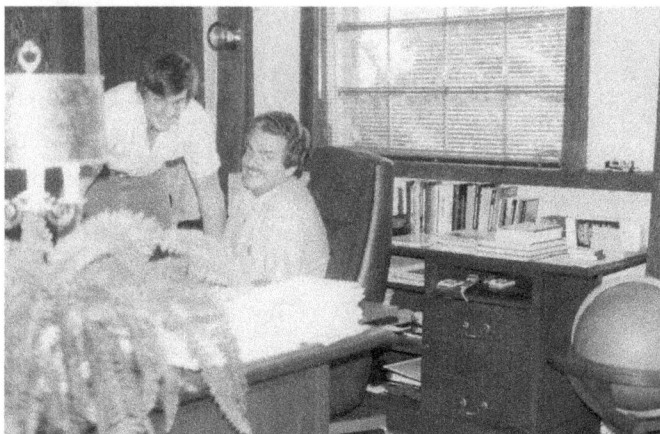

1980 | Bernard in Bob's office. On the photo back:
"No mon. No fun. Your son.
Too bad. I'm sad. Your Dad."

am I going to do?" As he was standing there weaving I said, "Have you been drinking?" and I felt my old fundamentalist presuppositions beginning to take control. In a moment of time, I saw that my real concern was not about *him;* I was worried about me and my reputation. I didn't want him to embarrass me. I was stunned by the realization that I would rather be right than truthful. He stood there defiant, and he said, "Yes! I have been drinking."

Here was the first father challenge; it was an opportunity for him to become his own man and distance himself from his strong father and become his own person. I yielded to whatever God the Father was doing in his life and responded, "Okay, go to bed." He was stunned.

A little while later I heard a knock on my door and he said, "Dad, I need to talk to you." We stood in the hallway and he said, "I didn't really want to drink. What I wanted to do was be *rebellious*." According to him he never drank that much again. I was required to see past the present circumstances and hold fast with confidence to that *incorruptible* seed that was in him. My thought, expressed like a prayer was, "Live, Seed, live!"

Legalism does not have the capacity to bring people to maturity. God gave us freedom of choice. His sovereignty and patience is expressed by His refusing to take it back. As a father, I had no choice but to give my 18-year-old son freedom and liberty to find his own way. What he did with it initially was go out and drink. Standing there in that doorway I reached for that freedom, seriously contemplating taking that freedom from him. It is almost irresistible for parents and spiritual leaders to control the urge to take someone's freedom back, but repeated rescue attempts deny people both the ability and the freedom to grow up.

During these years, three particular doctrines or points of understanding became clear to me:

1. *Personal responsibility.* Teaching people to be *responsible* for their own life is difficult. Biblical responsibility has nearly disappeared from Western civilization. We will not know for another 50 years how much damage Sigmund Freud caused by shifting blame from ourselves to others. Then Marx came with

his economic determinism causing every human being to see themselves as victims, allowing us to break loose from our moorings of personal responsibility. We live in a day of relativism, re-assignment of cause, and constant shift of blame to others. There is an absence of *content* in meaning. Restoring this seems nearly impossible apart from a miracle of God. Few are desirous, let alone capable, of taking responsibility for their own actions because the modern philosophy is to run, hide, and shift blame!

2. *Personal accountability.* The Scripture says very clearly that leaders should be *accountable* not only to God but to other leaders. When we use the word "accountability," many fear legalism. My point is simply that *because* every person is a redeemed sinner, every person, including leaders, needs to be accountable. A person called forth in ministry still has the Kingdom treasure in an earthen vessel (see 2 Cor. 4:7) or as I like to put it, a Styrofoam cup, and they remain very human. However anointed, charismatic, and persuasive they may be with strength, power, or spiritual insight, their human nature remains. May I suggest that if you do not have someone to whom you are accountable, seek God, ask Him to show you where it is that you can give account (see Luke 9:10). Someone whom you trust who could help you live by the plain meaning of Scripture.

3. *Seeing things governmentally.* If we ever have our eyes opened to the Kingdom of God, it will cause us to understand that Jesus is actually a real King. He is

identified in Acts as "another King, one Jesus!" (Acts 17:7). His government is real. It may be essentially spiritual, it is none-the-less ultimate reality. Thus, when we pray for "His will to be done on the earth as it is in heaven" (Matt. 6:10), it will change our outlook. When we see the New Testament governmentally, we also see that elders, apostles, prophets, pastors, teachers, and evangelists are also *governmental.* How we receive and respond to them makes a great difference in the manner in which God responds to us. John 13:20 says, "Truly, truly, I say to you, he who receives whomever I send receives Me; and he who receives Me receives Him who sent Me."

1984 revealed the painful breakup of the five teachers. Knowing I needed to be accountable to someone, I chose to renew my relationship with Elim Fellowship once again. The faithfulness of those who had ordained me was evident by their love, support, and correction during the years of conflict surrounding the Discipleship controversy. In 1987, I wrote a national apology for the extremes and injuries that occurred in an attempt to heal and restore those who remained confused and concerned. This was well received by most and began to bring healing and reconciliation. However, the controversy took a great toll on me personally. My physical and emotional health began to suffer. I experienced exhaustion, burnout, and disappointment in wishing it could have been different. Thirty years of travel, spiritual warfare, and unrelenting pressures had taken its predictable toll. I burned up all my adrenaline and was running on fumes. Paul said it best when he described the principle and cost of feeding God's people: "So death works in us, but life in you" (2 Cor. 4:12).

Toxicity

In 1987, I was in Sweden with a large group of business executives. I wasn't feeling well so when I finished ministering I went upstairs. The muscles in my stomach, thighs, and arms began to shake drastically and I started on a serious physical journey. My first doctor was in San Francisco and he put on his rubber gloves and his white coat and began to treat me strangely. I thought, *"What's wrong with him?"* Then I realized that he thought I had AIDS. So, I went to another doctor and after a whole pile of exams he thought I had early stages of Alzheimer's. Suddenly, I had a mental image of myself as a little old man on a sun porch and said to him, "Forgive me, but that's not true." He suggested I get another doctor and I said, "That's exactly what I had in mind!" I refused

1987 | Bob Mumford

that diagnosis on faith alone. By about the 8th doctor I received the diagnosis of a toxic reaction to mercury and lead. But I could not find a doctor to treat me. I even saw a doctor at Duke University Hospital who gave me all kinds of tests then dismissed me. All the doctors were afraid of being sued because they didn't know how to treat me so, instead of me leaving them, they're leaving me.

In the middle of this, I felt the Lord say that the lead and mercury were like some kind of infection in the body of Christ. I didn't feel like a martyr, but I did feel like I was living out something prophetic. The symptoms were physical shaking, loss of memory and tremendous exhaustion and I was deeply challenged. I would get up, take my shower, and want to go back to bed. Because lead and mercury are both tasteless and odorless, they are difficult to identify but are in a wide variety of foods. The physical body does not have the capacity to handle mercury and so I began a series of intravenous treatments to purge it out of my system.

The further I got into this, the further I withdrew from everyone. I was moving more and more toward a prophetic cave where I could hide out and nurse my wounds. I said to the Lord, "I'd like to have a German Shepherd and 5 acres of land and teach the German Shepherd to bite anybody who carries a Bible." I became critical and mean and very difficult to live with.

All this started in 1987 and by 1991, I was sitting on the back porch very early in the morning and was angry at the Lord. I yelled, "Lord, what do You want from me? Get off my back!"

He responded, "I want your unshared love."

I was stunned He even responded. A while later, He asked me, "Do you want to know Me?" Since the day I got saved My prayer has always been "I want to know You!" (Phil. 3:10). As soon as I learned that verse as a new Christian, it has been the prayer of my life. I have always wanted to know Him. I responded, "Yes! I want to know You!"

He said, "I want you to decide whether you want to know Me experientially or know Me through the Scriptures?" I have always longed for the Lord to step out of the closet and say, "Hey, its Me, God!" but I learned that overmuch presence of God becomes compulsive and it isn't real love. We often respond because we're afraid of Him. And so I wrestled through this and finally said to the Father, "I want to know You through the Scriptures."

In the midst of my physical issues, the Scriptures began to open to me in ways they never had before. I began to see His character and what He's like and fell in love with Him all over again. After about 10 years, He began coming to me experientially again. God is *Agape* and I was seeing *Agape* in action in a whole new way.

I was on a crowded airplane just after the twin towers collapsed in 2001 and the atmosphere was tense. Boarding the plane was a nervous, young Muslim mother all dressed in her garb carrying a little baby boy. I thought, *Lord, let me practice Agape on this kid.* I could feel the warm love of God rise in me and reach out to that child. The mother was standing next to me in the packed aisle so I said to her, "Your baby is beautiful." I'm not all that great to look at, but when the mother turned around to me, the baby gave me a smile like a Cheshire cat. He locked onto me and I thought he was going to climb out of his mother's arms into mine. When the *Agape* of God reached out from me and touched her child, the mother smiled. I thought *I've only been at this 50 years and I'm just now starting to understand the Gospel.* I was deeply moved because I saw that all of God's creation responds to His love. Creation waits for love. If Christ is formed in us, the world sees *Agape.*

There is deep conviction in me that a person who is spiritually healthy should be *comfortable in the presence of God.* It seems like a simple goal, but most of us are not comfortable in the presence of God. We feel our guilt, our failure, our inadequacy, or we are anxious about things that we did or didn't do. One of the goals that I strive for in teaching is to lift people from where they are, seeking to bring them into the presence of God in a way that enables them to be comfortable and enjoy the Lord.

My desire was to find a place to recover and prepare for the next few years of God's unfolding purpose. Through a series of leadings, we moved our Lifechangers' office to Raleigh, North Carolina, a place that proved to be God's city of refuge for us as a ministry and as a family.

Financially and spiritually, the Lord has abundantly provided friends and underwriters that have faithfully stood with us even through God's pruning and cultivating me for the purpose of more fruit. For each of you, I am deeply thankful and personally humbled.

Following Jesus

For the past 60 years, the Lord has emphasized in my own life the skill of following Jesus. I believe that Jesus would rather have us simply follow Him than be overly concerned about our spiritual condition. My emphasis in teaching has been to show others *how to follow Jesus.* When the Lord forcibly instructed me to *slow down* and significantly reduce ministry and travel ten years ago, I used the time to study the Gospels. I wanted to know Him through Scripture so I read and reread the Gospels. I listened to the four Gospels on CD for hours at a time and heard things I had not grasped in reading. Through my own struggles to live my life in a manner that was pleasing to the Father, I was able to share with thousands of people, as personally and vulnerably as I knew how, the lessons I've learned. Out of this came messages such as *The Implications of Following Jesus, Giving God What He Seeks, Mouthful of Splinters, The Real You,* and *Bent Knee Society.* As you can tell from the titles, the Lord had been working me over! Teaching others what the Lord taught me has been challenging, and as I have shared faithfully with others, their lives have been changed, too.

The hours of studying the Gospels were a joy; His instruction to *reduce ministry* was painful. It caused severe withdrawal symptoms. I would often rationalize the acceptance of ministry invitations even after He had given direction to shut it down. But the Lord has His ways and means committee and slowly got my full attention!

My commission for the next few years was to write what He put on my heart. With great difficulty, I turned down many important ministry invitations around the world. The Lord seemed to be pressing me to give a permanent record of what He taught me over the last 60 years. I know that books, when read, promote action and form opinions for generations to come. My daughter, Keren, who has been working with me for many years began writing my life message, which has to do with practical application of the Christian walk. We worked on the books *The Agape*

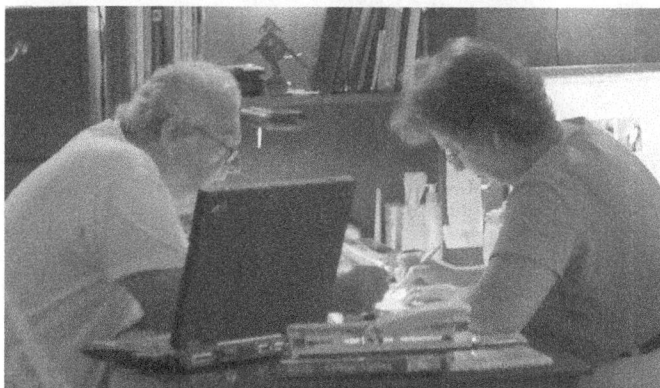

2006 | Bob and Keren working together

Road, The Mysterious Seed, and *Nourishing the Seed.* It was an exciting adventure and an ultimate challenge to capture what the Lord has given and explain it on paper. Keren is working on a few more books that are in me, including *The Victorious Seed,* which is in the works, and I especially look forward to working on one that interprets the Kingdom of God as I've come to see it in Scripture. My prayer is that I will be faithful and pleasing to the Lord in all things.

Change of Command

At 77 years old, I began to discover the inability to make the hard decisions necessary for the success of the Lifechangers ministry. I felt strongly that I was to ask our son, Eric, to consider taking the leadership of the ministry. I remembered taking Eric on a trip

2007 | Eric and Bob studying together

with me to Toronto when he was 9 years old. I sat on a chair in the hotel room and Eric climbed up on the bed and as I tried to explain to him the prophetic commissioning I felt from the Lord. I felt like David as a man of war and his son Solomon who was a man of peace. David prepared the material for the temple, but Solomon was to build it. I unloaded my deepest feelings into this 9-year-old without any assurance that he understood or had even heard me. He was listening to me but was restless and jiggling, looking at the ceiling, at his shoes, and at the TV wishing it was on. Now, here we are, years later, and he has more than picked up the teaching commission which I carried.

Eric decided to move the office from Raleigh to Cookeville, Tennessee where office space was more reasonable and where he had been pastoring and had

2012 | Mark & Julie Duggin, Steve & Shoni Smith

a strong support base. Mark and Julie Duggin along with Steve and Shoni Smith took responsibility for operations and have been more than faithful stewards to carry the vision; they have become yoked with us on this journey.

All our children have sought to make the journey into the Kingdom dimension with us. Family support has been a life-saving factor for our 60-year journey. I remember our daughter, Keren, who at age 12 fell in the bed of the truck and broke her arm while stacking New Wine Magazines. Keren has labored with me with diligence and faithfulness since the inception of Lifechangers in 1972. She has been my assistant, effective editor, has put into writing the content of all the *Plumblines* and more than 20 books, and has helped with all of my teaching notes and presentations.

2012 | Keren, Bernard, Bob, Judith, Eric, and Beth

And now with joy, she finds herself doing the same for her brother, Eric, on his powerful writings. Keren and her husband Michael live in Denver, Colorado near their two children and three grandchildren.

Our daughter, Beth, left her career in business to become the office manager of Lifechangers for more than five years. She then got her degree as a licensed counselor and finds herself helping deeply hurting families. She and her husband, J.R. live near us in Raleigh along with her two daughters and two grandchildren. Her son, James, and his wife, Paula, and their 4 children live in Australia where he pastors.

For many years, our son Bernard traveled with me to quite a few countries. He started his own furniture restoration business, Mumford Restoration, in San Francisco, then moved the company and his family to Raleigh 21 years ago and is thriving. He has eight amazing children, two of them adopted—one from Guatemala and the other from Ethiopia. We enjoy getting together with them on a weekly basis.

Eric lives on two continents. He stays with Cory and Laurel Siffring in Kingsport, Tennessee while in the U.S. and he and Suzanne live at Father's House in Kampala, Uganda with their 18 children whom they home school. They are quite active hosting medical mission teams, doing work in the Namowango Slum, and a colorful variety of other activities the Lord calls them to, facilitating the children in sports and art and outreach to the community. Their two daughters are in college in Tennessee and New York.

God has blessed Judith and me with four very different children and as families, we so enjoy sharing life together.

Summary

From 1954 to 2014 is 60 years in active ministry. It began in that little four-bed sick bay on the USS *Aludra* when I began to embrace the call to teach. Feeding God's people in every nation has been my commission. Now Eric is carrying more than his portion of the burden of our Kingdom proclamation and has done so with integrity and vision. All that he is opening on the nature of the Trinity and fusion oneness is taking on an importance that seems increasingly vital as we seek to face the changes and complexities of our present day.

One day, not so long ago, while reading my Greek New Testament I suddenly realized that Father had heard and answered my prayer as a new believer in the Navy to be able to read the New Testament in Greek. I went to Bible College, then finished my B.A. at University of Delaware in Wilmington, then enrolled in Seminary, and a few years later was reading First John in Greek. The illumination of Father's faithfulness caused me to weep and rejoice. God, as a heavenly Father, set His choice on a small street kid from the other side of the tracks, moving me towards my destiny I now know as THAT. If He can do it with a street kid, He can do it with you and with those whom you are seeking to share this Good News of the Kingdom. Maturity in the body of Christ depends on each of us discovering and being loyal to the process of moving towards our destiny. May we not tire and become weary of the journey; His purpose and intent is more than worthy of our uninterrupted abiding.

Thank you for allowing me to make this journey with you. If Judith and I and our family have contributed something to encourage or strengthen you when you were weary or perhaps helped solve something that *appeared* unsolvable, we are deeply grateful.

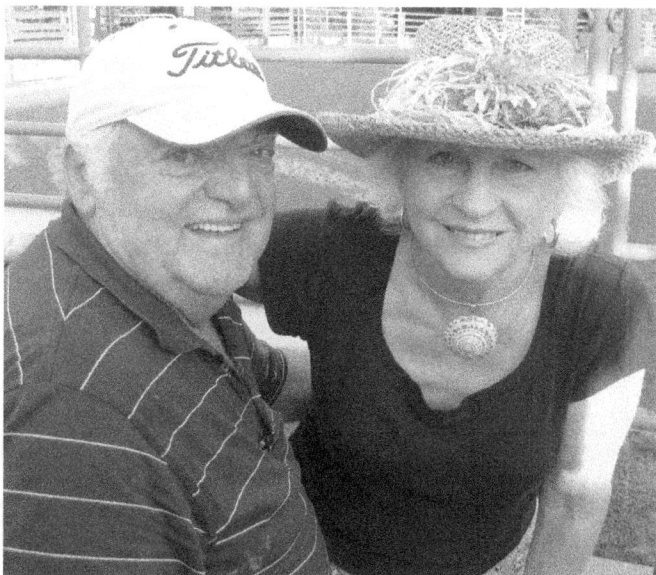

Bob Mumford

Grace
by Bob Mumford

Father of this,
  and the life to come —
Who knows all hearts,
  and dwells in some;
To you I write
  this poem of love,
And know by the Spirit
  it will reach above

I like many
  have failed to do
All the things
  we've seen of you.
Yet in thy Word
  in print so clear,
I've read these words
  I hold so dear

"By GRACE are ye saved ...
  through faith in me!
You lack so much,
  but I'll add to thee.
My righteousness
  won't come by force —
I require that
  you know the source."

Now when I stumble,
   and often fall,
"hold, Oh hold my hand!"
   I call.
Desiring with Thee
   in love to abide;
I know I've felt
   your strength provide.

And when in providence
   you permit a test;
The Tempter tries
   from you to wrest;
I know, I know
   that you can see,
And through this
   prove your love for me.

In the world to come,
   as we look back,
We'll see much sin,
   our hearts as black.
But this O Lord,
   as I see through,
Pleases Thee
   and makes our debt to you.
      —Ephesians 2:7-9

Written February, 1957

Materials by Bob Mumford

Books

Agape Road
Dr. Frankenstein and World Systems
Entering and Enjoying Worship
Fifteen Steps Out
The King and You
Living Happily Ever After
Mysterious Seed
Nourishing the Seed
Prison of Resentment
Problem of Doing Your Own Thing
Take Another Look at Guidance
Purpose of Temptation

Booklets

Acting Against Myself
Becoming a Father Pleaser
Being Bilingual
Being Scandalized
Below the Bottom Line
Burnt Stones
Change in the Wind
Church of My Dreams
Conscience & Confidence
Correction Not Rejection
Corn of Wheat
Difference Between the Church and the Kingdom
Escape from Christendom
Forever Change
Gang of Ugly Facts

Psalm for Living
Pulling the Kings Carriage
Renegade Male
Rewards of Faithfulness
Rewards of Waiting on God
Riddle of the Painful Earth
Sitting in Darkness, Walking in Light
Spiritual Paternity
Standing in the Whirlwind
Surrendering Ungoverned Desires
Ten Words & Ungoverned Desires
Three Dimensional Reality
Transforming Human Behavior
Trap, Exit and Reward
Water Baptism
When God Changed His Address
Why God?

Bible Studies

Agape Road
Arena of Truth
Breaking Out (in Spanish)
Knowing, Loving Following Jesus
Motivation: From Frustration to Joy
Unshared Love

In addition, Bob has written hundreds of magazine articles and recorded over 500 spoken messages.

www.ingramcontent.com/pod-product-compliance
Lightning Source LLC
Chambersburg PA
CBHW061748020426
42331CB00006B/1396